Mother of the Groom

ALSO BY SHARON NAYLOR

Mother
of the
Groom

**Everything You Need
to Know to Enjoy
the Best Wedding Ever**

Sharon Naylor

CITADEL PRESS
Kensington Publishing Corp.
www.kensingtonbooks.com

CITADEL PRESS books are published by

Kensington Publishing Corp.
850 Third Avenue
New York, NY 10022

All Kensington titles, imprints, and distributed lines are available at special quantity discounts for bulk purchases for sales promotions, premiums, fund-raising, educational, or institutional use. Special book excerpts or customized printings can also be created to fit specific needs. For details, write or phone the office of the Kensington special sales manager: Kensington Publishing Corp., 850 Third Avenue, New York, NY 10022, attn: Special Sales Department; phone 1-800-221-2647.

CITADEL PRESS and the Citadel logo are Reg. U.S. Pat. & TM Off.

First printing: April 2005
First paperback printing: January 2006

10   9   8   7

Printed in the United States of America

Library of Congress Control Number: 2004095833

ISBN 0-8065-2645-9

For my own mother

Joanne Blahitka

And for my grandmother Rose

Contents

Preface

CONGRATULATIONS! Your son is getting married! As he takes on a new title, groom-to-be, you also take on a new title of your own: mother of the groom. And as he finds himself in a brand-new role with a long list of duties and responsibilities, so, too, do you. You and he might not have had a lot in common over the years, but right now you're in the same boat. You're sharing the planning of a wedding and a major life change. He's preparing to be a husband, and you're preparing to be a mother-in-law. He's living in a world that revolves around the wedding, and so too are you. The moment he slipped that ring onto his fiancée's finger, *your* life changed forever, as well. It's exciting, and at times overwhelming. You're filled with happiness for your son and his bride-to-be! There's so much to look forward to—and do!

You couldn't be in a better position, timing-wise. Just a few years ago, the mother of the groom had very little to do with the wedding plans. The bride and her mother took care of just about everything (since her parents were paying for the wedding), and the mother of the groom got to plan only the rehearsal dinner . . . and pick out her own dress for the wedding. As time went on, brides started inviting their prospective mothers-in-law to help with a few plans—from participating in the cake tasting to choosing the wedding cake, and helping to make the favors—and thus started a growing trend of bringing in the mother of the groom for tasks that were traditionally shared by the dynamic duo of weddings: the bride and *her* mom.

Now that we're in the twenty-first century, and brides are somewhat older and more established in their own lives, their parents are not necessarily handed the wedding-planning reins. Brides and grooms are more often paying for their own weddings, doing the lion's share of the planning themselves, and *all* of the parents are given minor supporting roles. That puts you on much the same level as the mother of the bride (and we'll get to how happy *she* is about that in just a while!).

The trends of weddings today reveal the shift: only a percentage of today's weddings are paid for and planned by the bride's family alone. A third of weddings are paid for and planned by the couple alone. And here's the big one . . .

Over half of today's weddings are planned by the bride and groom, together with the bride's family *and* the groom's family.

"Over half" may not seem like an overwhelming majority, but it's huge when you think about the fact that just a few years ago, this number was in the single digits. Clearly, right now is *the* time to be a mother of the groom, since you're very likely to have a big role in the planning process. That's why I've decided to write a book just for *you* right now. *The Mother of the Bride* guide that I wrote a few years ago is out there on bookshelves and helping thousands of moms navigate the sometimes rough waters of wedding planning; now since the mother of the groom has a much bigger role and many more responsibilities, it's *your* turn.

This is your time, too.

You have in your hands the book that is going to help *you* navigate the sometimes rough waters of wedding planning, made all the more difficult by those changing roles—both moms are now sharing the spotlight. This book will guide you through the many details of planning the big event, with new information you need about the wedding industry. (Things have changed a *lot* since you planned your wedding!) And even more important: You'll find good advice on creating positive new relationships with your son, his bride, and her family. *That's* the biggest responsibility you have, even if it seems like finding a location for the reception and choosing napkin colors are the big issues right now. So take notes, use the checklists to keep you organized, and this wedding will turn out to be the time of your life as well.

There's so much to look forward to in the months ahead . . . so get ready to have fun, to work as part of a team for something wonderful for your son and his bride, and to look absolutely *gorgeous* on the wedding day. It all begins right now . . .

Acknowledgments ⌁

WITH HEAPS OF THANKS TO . . .

- My editor Bruce Bender at Kensington for once again taking me on and helping to create a useful tool for the mother of the "happiest couple in the world."

- Margaret Wolf at Citadel for her terrific attention to detail and support.

- My fabulous and fashionable agent Meredith Bernstein for once again bringing me a wonderful opportunity on a fun subject.

- Scott Buhrmaster, who is a genius and a mentor, a dream of a publicist.

- The many insightful and extraordinarily talented wedding professionals who shared their ideas with me (and now, with you).

- My family and friends, who are a part of everything I create.

- And to Madison and Kevin, my little angels.

PART ONE

Pre-Planning

CHAPTER 1

Let the Celebrations Begin!

YOU MAY HAVE KNOWN it was coming. Perhaps you knew your son bought the engagement ring, and you were in on the secret that he's been hiding that little velvet ring box in his sock drawer for the past two months. Maybe he even solicited your advice as he planned the proposal to his bride-to-be. ("Fill the room with white roses and pillar candles, and don't forget to get down on one knee! Chivalry counts!") It's then a waiting game until your son and his new fiancée burst through your front door, glowing and radiant as they share their wonderful news with you. The ring hasn't even been on the bride-to-be's finger for a full day yet, and here she is holding out her hand as if she had a fresh manicure, hardly able to speak coherently. The excitement is palpable and contagious. Soon, there are tears in your eyes too, and *you're* so excited you can't speak either.

This is a special moment. There are few in life so electrically charged with pure happiness and joy. So, that means it's time to celebrate.

Sharing with Bride and Groom

If you *were* in the know . . . if you were privy to the date, time, and place of your son's proposal and have just been waiting at home, watching the clock, for the newly engaged couple to come through that door, then you might have prepared for a welcome celebration. Perhaps you chilled a top-notch bottle of champagne, spent the day making a delicious meal, or stopped in at the bakery for a cake. Time to fire up the espresso machine, and it's a party!

If the surprise was kept even from you, then be spontaneous! Call your other kids to come over, load everyone into cars, and go out to dinner! (By the way, if the "big moment" has already passed and you didn't celebrate immediately, it's not too late. Call the couple and take them out for a congratulatory meal or drinks now.)

Whenever and however your first celebration with the happy couple takes place, go the extra mile and make it special. Bring flowers for the bride-to-be (she

---

I Can't Wait to Tell *Everyone* the Good News!

Stop right there! Put the phone down! This will save you from making a truly terrible move and ruining *everything* by getting off on the worst foot possible with the bride and groom. Many newly engaged couples fear that their parents are going to take over the things *they* want to do. They may be very excited about calling the relatives to share their good news. If you do it first—without their knowledge—it's stealing their thunder, and can potentially embarrass them when they call up Grandma and say "Guess what?!" when Grandma already knows. It may sound trivial, but trust me . . . the minute an engagement ring is in play, it's exactly this kind of "trivial" thing that can cause the biggest blowups and power struggles. Play it safe before you call everyone; *ask the bride and groom* who they'd like to inform and who you can call. You won't believe how appreciative they'll be of this simple, respectful step. Right now, at Minute One, you're giving them a tremendously important message: I'm going to defer to you, since I realize this is your wedding. That's the best and smartest way to start off, and it will get you far in this entire process. *Then* you can call everyone you know.

---

might have a bouquet for you, too!), make your son's favorite meal (the one he requests for his birthday dinners). Choose the best Hallmark card out there and inscribe your most heartfelt wishes, congratulations, and perhaps even a gem of advice from Mom. From this moment on, every special touch you offer becomes part of their forever-cherished memories of the best time of their life together.

Remember, this first celebration with the couple doesn't have to be an all-out, expensive affair. There will be plenty of pricey, fancy parties later (like the rehearsal dinner). This is a celebration with more heart than art, more personality than price. It can be cocktails by your home hearth, drinks at a jazz club, even a laid-back backyard barbecue. All that matters is that it reflects a sense of home and family to the groom and his new bride-to-be.

Meet the Folks

In today's wedding scenarios, the couple's sets of parents might have already met, and may be close friends already who socialize as if the bride and groom are already married. Or, since we do live in a global society where a bride from one state might be marrying a groom from another state (or country!), the parents might not have met in advance of the wedding plans. In the case of truly international love stories, they might not even meet until the wedding weekend.

If the engagement means that you'll be meeting the bride's family for the first time, this is an important celebration. The bride and groom are bringing their two sides of the future family together, as you're all going to be one big happy family . . . hopefully. We'll get into the challenges of working with the bride's family in the next chapter, but for now we'll deal with the celebration at hand. You're going to be partners with the bride's family. Not just for the wedding, but for every blessing to come in the future: your grandchildren, the couple's new homes, trading off holidays spent together. These other parents, the bride's parents, are going to be in your life, so here's where you start off *that* new relationship with a flourish.

Before any of the big, official engagement celebrations begin, even if you've known the bride's family for years, it's a wonderful idea to have a special celebration dinner with the couple, the bride's family, and all of the bride's and groom's siblings. Call this an "inner circle" party where the wine can flow, and you all can bask in the glow of the couple's great news together before the preliminary discussions of wedding plans, budgeting, and who's going to do what for the wedding. It will get *crazy* very soon, so take the initiative to gather close family together for a shared celebration dinner. Ideas for this gathering include:

* Informal at-home dinner, cooked by you
* Informal at-home dinner, catered
* Dinner out at a formal restaurant
* Dinner out at a family-style restaurant
* Dinner out at a sushi restaurant
* Dinner out at a tapas restaurant (very hot right now!)
* Dinner out at a fondue restaurant (also very hot right now!)
* Dessert and champagne party at your house
* Wine and cheese party at your house
* Brunch out at a restaurant, or catered/homemade at your house
* Drinks at a jazz club

Make the setting, meal, and celebration something different, something that will please the guests and make this an occasion to remember.

And yes, *after* this dinner is when the first official planning conversations might take place, especially if you or the bride's parents have had to travel far to attend, and this is the best and most efficient time to set the foundation for the wedding plans with everyone face to face. So enjoy the celebration, and then move on to start talking about how the couple wishes to divide the wedding plans among everyone, how budget will be handled, and also—most important— so the bride and groom can share with you the their wedding ideas. Will it be outdoors? A destination wedding? A traditional wedding? This meeting is where you will find out. Some tips to ensure that it goes smoothly (share these with the groom's father and any stepparents if that applies, so that they may go into this meeting well-prepared for the diplomacy required):

- Ask the bride and groom to begin sharing their wishes for and plans about the wedding.

- Offer your ideas when asked.

- Remember that body language speaks louder than words. If you don't like what you're hearing—from the couple or from the bride's parents—just remain neutral. You can speak with the bride and groom later. Eye-rolling or obvious signs of impatience or frustration (especially if you're not so fond of the bride's parents, which can be the case) will only create problems.

Again, flip to chapter 2 for all you need to know about working with others. I wanted you to be prepared for some "shop talk" at this initial celebration, but otherwise the mood should be celebratory, relaxed, and tension-free. If others seem to be stepping over the line, you can win big sainthood points by interrupting to steer the occasion back to its true nature: a party. Time for dessert!

Engagement Parties

Traditionally, and even with the big shift in who's planning and paying for weddings these days, the bride's family usually handles the engagement party—that is, if you're all living in the same geographical area. If they're in one state, they can have their own engagement party for the couple, and you can hold a separate engagement party with your own guest list. Dual parties in your own time zones mean that the bride and groom's bridal party members from both regions can more easily attend a celebration in the couple's honor.

The style and formality of the party you give is, of course, up to you. Some parents of the groom love being able to host a formal party in their homes, or out at a restaurant or hotel ballroom. There's also plenty of more informal party-giving such as backyard barbecues or picnics at a local park, something easier on the wallet. You do have a wedding to plan, after all.

Etiquette Alert!

Before you plan your engagement party, be *sure* the bride and groom have their official wedding guest list set in stone. They've taken your list of guest names, they've taken the bride's family's list, and they now have their master list and their final head count for all the guests who will be invited to their wedding. You must *not* invite anyone to an engagement party who will not be invited to the wedding: It's not only bad form, but it can be an extremely hurtful insult.

The only exception to the above mandate is in the case of an elopement or a destination wedding where only a small handful of guests will be invited. In these two cases alone, a separate reception can be held for the masses *after the wedding has taken place.* This is one of those new rules of weddings . . . couples do want to celebrate with all of their loved ones, and they are perfectly within bounds of proper behavior having a celebration after the fact. But it is now—and always will be—bad etiquette to invite guests to an engagement party if they won't be invited to the wedding. Case closed.

That said, you should also know that many brides and grooms choose *not* to have an engagement party. They might see it as an unnecessary burden on their guests if they ask them to block off time in their busy schedules, travel, and buy a gift for this official party. For some couples, it's just too much, and they really don't want or need an official engagement party. It's enough that they celebrated with their closest family and bridal party members, and that the shower and the rehearsal dinner are still to come. So, again, before you start to plan an engagement party, be sure it's something the bride and groom want.

Newspaper Announcements

Submitting the couple's official engagement photo and brief bios to the local newspaper used to be *the* big way to share the good news. Most couples stick with tradition and submit their basic information via the newspaper's semi-strict format and somewhat bland wording for all the town to see, but many *more* couples these days are taking the public announcement a big leap further. They're going online . . .

Wedding Web Sites

Oprah has her own Web site. So does Bed Bath & Beyond. And now your son and his bride can be the stars of their own personalized, all-about-us wedding Web site. They can create their own site featuring their official engagement portrait *plus* additional photos of themselves from the night of the engagement, their baby pictures, snapshots from vacations, and so on. They can post the story of how they met, how they fell in love, how your son proposed. They can even arrange the site to play a video of the actual proposal. It's the twenty-first-century answer to the wedding announcement, with special effects and all. And you can help make it happen for them. More and more parents of brides and grooms are buying the happy couple a year's worth of wedding Web site service, where they can share their stories and all the must-have information the guests will need. It's a keepsake and a planning tool, not to mention the best way possible for them to share their wedding news with their far-flung friends and family.

Check out www.wedstudio.com, one of the top sites where couples can build, design, write, and post their own wedding Web sites. WedStudio.com's vice president, Krista Meikle, has this to say about what such a site can do for the couple: "Wedding Web sites are a great way for brides and grooms to announce their engagement and upcoming wedding. A personal wedding Web site by WedStudio.com provides the bride and groom with the ability to share their traditions and special moments as well as providing one place for all of their friends and family to enjoy." With a WedStudio Web site, the bride and groom can:

- **Announce:** Tell friends and family they're engaged and getting married.
- **Inform:** Give guests the information they need to ensure a stress-free visit.

- **Share:** Post photographs and share special moments with loved ones.
- **RSVP:** Save time and money by getting RSVPs online.
- **Connect:** Provide local city, hotel, and site contact information for out-of-town guests to arrange their travel plans.
- **Register:** Link to online retailers and provide guests easy access to registries.

"WedStudio.com, a leading provider of personal wedding Web sites, makes it easy for even those that are not so computer savvy to purchase a wedding Web site subscription as a gift. It's as simple as filling out a form, and then WedStudio will e-mail your gift to the recipient."

Throughout the coming months of planning, this Web site will be a fun place for the bride and groom to record all the goings-on, a great way for their friends to share in their joy, and also a monumental timesaver and stress reliever—you *won't* have to provide directions and details to the 150 people on the guest list, individually or through a mass mailing. The guests just go to the site, point and click, and they find all the directions and information they need. They can contact the hotel to request a crib for their room; they can find the bride's registry information. Simple as that. No worries for you or for the bride and groom.

Even better, my recent survey said that of the 80 percent of today's grooms participating and partnering in the wedding plans, most of the men said they loved creating and managing the wedding Web site, updating it, posting new photos . . . using their hi-tech smarts to show their enthusiasm about the wedding (and the bride) as they were never able to before. So if you give the bride and groom their own Web site to enjoy and share, you may also be giving the groom a place to shine.

Celebrating on Your Own

The happy couple has left the building and now comes a warm and wonderful moment during which you can share a private toast with the groom's father. After all, this is the start of a new phase in *your* lives. You've done a wonderful job raising your son, and he's about to embark on a fabulous adventure.

Congratulations, Mom. Here's a toast to you as well.

CHAPTER 2

Where Do You Come In?

So, where do I begin? you might be wondering.

Even though you know mothers of the groom are more involved in the planning process, the exact size and scope of your role, your exact assignments and responsibilities, will be determined by the bride and groom. This is true even if you're paying for a good chunk of the wedding.

That's right . . . the old adage sung by many a later-resented parent, the battle cry of "I'm paying for it, so I make the decisions" is gone, gone, gone. Today's brides and grooms are not kids, and they'll just as likely cut you out of the entire planning process if you try such a time-honored power play. It just doesn't work anymore.

Today's mothers of the groom are far more gracious and respectful. Even if they've contributed a boatload of cash for the wedding, they know it's the bride and groom's day to plan. Since *you're* gracious and respectful, your response is going to be a good-natured "How can I help?"

I can't emphasize enough that deferring to the couple is key.

Here's where you will *all* work out who will do what for the wedding and everything leading up to it. You're setting the foundation—a solid foundation—for the process ahead of you, so that it will turn out fabulously in the end. Right here is where the bride and groom, you, the mother of the bride, the fathers and various stepparents perhaps all sit down to break down the enormous wedding-planning task into bite-size pieces, each planning detail dealt out to the eagerly waiting hands of the parents. But be forewarned: Things can get a little bit tricky.

Beware of *the Spell*

People can get very possessive and territorial over who gets to handle certain wedding tasks—often the high-profile ones, like the cake and the entertainment, the things the guests will notice most. I've seen sets of parents who got along like best friends for years suddenly turn into snarling pit bulls brawling over something as simple as ordering the wedding favors (i.e., "It has to be traditional candy-coated almonds for good luck!" "No, it has to be Godiva chocolate! It's elegant!" "Oh, so your precious elegance means more than our family tradition?!" "You are a terrible person!" "No, you are a terrible person!" Usually, they don't say "terrible person" but something more colorful—you get the picture.) Veins throb, voices are raised higher, and hands are clenched, as former allies start snatching assignments away from each other like they're playing the Road Rage version of Go Fish. Everyone loses their minds over who gets "the best assignment" and who's stuck with "the raw deal." And the bride and groom sit there stupefied while their parents turn their wedding plans into a game of high-stakes poker.

It's like a spell descends upon them. Afterward, stumbling out to their cars after the irate groom and the tearful bride have thrown the bickering parents out, they think . . . "What happened back there? I can't believe I lost my mind like that." *That's* the Spell.

Weddings have a way of making even the calmest person—mother or bride—transform. In the media, they call this new creature Bridezilla or Momzilla, and neither one is a pretty sight. So what's the solution? How do you prevent such a metamorphosis? It's a two-shot solution: preparation and understanding, with a dash of good communication thrown on top.

Here's where you all start to prepare, so that you understand what the bride and groom want, and open up the doors to good communication as you make the first important decisions for the wedding.

What Do You Bring to the Table?

Before the bride and groom can even begin to decide who will do what, know that they want you to take care of the good stuff, and they want you to enjoy it. But first, they need to know what you're good at and what you'd most want to do. Consider this story from Dina, a recent bride from Connecticut:

> *We were trying to figure out who would order the wedding programs, my mother or his mother. We knew my mom really wanted that job, so we gave it to her. She found a few designs online, e-mailed us three of them, and we selected a nice one with calla lilies on it. I found out later that his mother has an artistic talent we weren't aware of. We knew she did watercolors at a class, she had all these gorgeous drawings in her office. But we had no idea that she had wanted to design our program covers but didn't want to step on my mom's toes for that job. If we had only known, it would have been so special to us and to her if we could have used her artwork for our programs!*

There's that communication thing! They have to know what you can offer so that you can offer your best. Here, to get you thinking about what you can "bring to the table" is a space for you to write out the things you're great at (crafts, using an online graphics program, keeping track of who needs to be paid and when, etc.):

Now, how do you convey this to the bride and groom without seeming like you're pushing for particular jobs? Just be direct, in an offering way. Whether via e-mail, phone, or an in-person conversation with the bride and groom, be sure to say "I'm there for whatever you need, but I wanted to remind you that I'm a whiz at calligraphy/cake decorating/mediating/contract review if you're looking for help with any of those things specifically." Put the ball in their court. Let them decide. You've made your offer and the best case for your talents.

What about the mother of the bride, who you can see is trying to run the show? It's tough to watch the bride get steamrolled by her mother, and it's tough to get flattened in her path when she decides to come after you trying to take your toy . . . or rather, your task. We'll get into that challenge more in chapter 3. For now, let's deal with your place in the wedding plans.

The bride will no doubt have her own books and lists of what needs to be done and who's paying for what. The following is a chart for your own tasks. On it, you'll record not only what you're responsible for but also who's taking care of other tasks. Why do you need to keep track of others' lists? It's all too easy to make an unintentional mistake by simply picking up a beautiful unity candle that you see in the craft store and then finding out that the mother of the bride is steaming mad that you have usurped her right, responsibility, and role as mother of the bride by taking over *her task* and aren't you just *a terrible person!* Huh? Trust me, it happens exactly like that. Remember the Spell.

So use the chart on the following pages to keep yourself and everyone else on the same page.

What's Not on the List

There are a few things that are not on the list that are hugely important tasks and responsibilities for you . . .

* Be the bride's partner. Listen to her. Let her know it's safe to talk with you about anything. Now is your time to bond with her and earn even more of her respect.

TASK	COUPLE	ME	MOTHER OF BRIDE	WEDDING COORDINATOR	OTHER
Engagement announcement					
Engagement party					
Wedding Web site					
Scouting ceremony sites					
Reserving ceremony site					
Scouting for wedding officiants					
Booking wedding officiant					
Ceremony décor					
Officiant's fee					
Marriage license					
Blood tests					
Pre-wedding counseling/classes					
Scouting for reception sites					
Booking reception site					
Rentals for reception site					
Preparation of reception site (landscaping, cleaning, and so on)					
Additional permits for parking, etc.					
Scouting for wedding gown					
Ordering wedding gown					
Wedding gown fittings					
Accessories and shoes					

TASK	COUPLE	ME	MOTHER OF BRIDE	WEDDING COORDINATOR	OTHER
Bride's manicure, pedicure, and hair					
Groom's clothing					
Groom's accessories					
Mothers' wardrobe search and purchase					
Men's clothing					
Men's accessories					
Children's wedding wardrobe selection and purchase					
Scouting for wedding coordinator					
Hiring wedding coordinator					
Scouting for invitations					
Wording for invitations					
Invitation layout on computer					
Postage					
Designing programs					
Creating programs					
Designing and creating other printed items (place cards, menu cards)					
Thank-you notes					
Scouting for caterers					
Going to tastings with caterer					
Arranging caterer's menu					
Liquor supply plans					

TASK	COUPLE	ME	MOTHER OF BRIDE	WEDDING COORDINATOR	OTHER
Shopping for liquor					
Scouting for cake designer					
Going for cake tastings					
Hiring cake designer and placing order					
Scouting for florist					
Creating flowers plan					
Ordering flowers					
Reception décor plans					
Hiring any extra reception décor experts					
Scouting for lighting director					
Planning seating chart for reception					
Filling out seating cards for guests					
Auditioning reception entertainment					
Hiring reception entertainment					
Scouting for photography expert					
Planning photography package					
Hiring photographer					
Scouting for videography expert					
Planning videography package					
Hiring videographer					
Buying wedding cameras					

TASK	COUPLE	ME	MOTHER OF BRIDE	WEDDING COORDINATOR	OTHER
Scouting for limousines or classic cars					
Booking limousines or classic cars					
Arranging other guest transportation					
Scouting for lodging for guests					
Booking lodging for guests					
Preparing guest welcome baskets					
Planning special events for guests at their hotel					
Buying or making favors					
Buying or making postceremony toss-its					
Scouting for rehearsal dinner locations and packages					
Booking the rehearsal dinner location					
Going for rehearsal dinner caterer tastings					
Booking the rehearsal dinner caterer					
Planning the rehearsal dinner menu					
Preparing food for the rehearsal dinner					
Buying and preparing rehearsal dinner favors and gifts					
Writing toasts and speeches for the wedding events					

TASK	COUPLE	ME	MOTHER OF BRIDE	WEDDING COORDINATOR	OTHER
Getting the bride and groom a gift					
Getting gifts for others					
Planning wedding weekend activities for out-of-town guests					
Hosting a bridal shower					
Scouting for honeymoon destination locations/packages					
Booking the honeymoon					
Scouting for the first-night honeymoon suite					
Booking the first-night honeymoon suite					
Arranging transportation for the bride and groom to the airport					
Arranging and paying tips					
Confirming with all wedding experts					
Other tasks:					
1.					
2.					
3.					
4.					
5.					
6.					
7.					
8.					
9.					
10.					

- Be a woman of your word. If you say you'll do something, do it and do it on time.

- Be accountable. If you can't do something on time, or if you're overwhelmed, be honest and let someone else help or take over.

- Be willing to compromise.

- Don't take on more than you can handle in an effort to be the "good mom" or to make others like you. Know your limits.

- Respect the budget at all times.

- Share with the father of the groom. He wants to be involved too, and not just as the person you vent to when things get stressful. Find something he can do.

- Put your own interpersonal tensions aside during this time. If your ex-husband has a new wife or girlfriend who's going to be a part of the wedding plans, find a way to peacefully coexist.

- Remember, it's an honor to help out with this wedding. A lot of other mothers have been on the other end of the wedding-planning trend, the one where the bride and groom take care of everything with no help or input from their families. So count your blessings for whatever you're asked to do and enjoy every moment.

Be Organized!

Whatever winds up on your To-Do list, remember to remain organized throughout the process. Create a folder or computer file for your wedding assignments, use your Palm Pilot, or sign up for free reminder services like those at www.hallmark.com or through your Internet program to keep you on track, on time, and on schedule. With so much going on, it's best to stay organized and so avert the wrath of the rest of the wedding-planning team!

CHAPTER 3

Works Well with Others

REMEMBER YOUR SON'S elementary school report card? The teacher would mark off "Satisfactory" or "Needs Improvement" for each of the areas in which the students were evaluated. *Plays Well with Others* was one of those areas.

Well, now it's your turn to be graded. How well do *you* work with others? You probably already know your own aptitude from your career life—how you partner up with colleagues, how you handle the boss's mood swings and whims, how you work under pressure hobbled by a particularly bossy co-worker who steals credit for your work or criticizes everything you do if it's not done his or her way.

Your work skills can help you in this wedding-planning process . . . *if* you have found good ways to deal with the abovementioned challenges. If not, then this process itself will be a learning experience and may perhaps even improve your work skills in the office. Fringe benefits.

Who You'll Be Working With

Here are the members of your team, many of whom can from time to time fall under the Spell:

The Bride
The Groom

The Mother of the Bride
The Father of the Bride
The Father of the Groom
Other Stepparents
The Wedding Coordinator

What was it they said about "too many cooks . . ."? Ask any sociologist or psychologist about group dynamics, and they can deliver a few hours' worth of group dynamic theories: "out of many, a leader must emerge," "two leaders will naturally clash until one emerges as the alpha," and "sides are often taken, and the collective IQ of the entire group can descend to the lowest common denominator." Of course, many of these experts have studied fourth-graders on the playground, but human instinct often follows these models. After all, millions of us watch "reality" TV to see the adult version of group dynamics at work, often at playground level. We watch the Discovery Channel to observe from the safety of our living rooms the socializing and power assertion rituals of orangutans and lions. The irony doesn't escape us when we see a mother bear howling with claws outstretched to protect her young. We're wired to protect our territory too.

Don't fear, we haven't called in the psychology department at Johns Hopkins or a team of physicists with their current chaos theories just yet. Your process has barely started. You probably haven't descended to the cutthroat level of middle-school playground mentality that can be the worst-case scenario of wedding planning. You've heard stories about it getting that bad. The bride's mother has threatened to boycott the wedding because the bride is consulting too much with the mother of the groom. The groom feels torn between his bride's wishes and his parents'. Everyone is saying nasty things about everyone else. One groom reported that the wedding planning had turned into a soap opera.

It's just a shame that people can sink so low as to make the wedding a drama, a sport, a place to flaunt their egos, bully, ridicule, and play mind games. And it can be prevented with the right lessons kept in mind at the beginning and repeated often throughout the process, especially when things get very tense right before the wedding. To repeat:

It's the bride and groom's wedding. Even if I'm paying for all or part of it, it's what they want that counts.

Ideally, the mother of the bride is also aware of this concept. Knowing this phrase and repeating it doesn't make you immune to the Spell. But it's a good reality check.

It's Not What You Think

Weddings are emotional events, and planning one is emotional as well. You'll certainly fall prey to some degree of the Spell from time to time. The bride will, everyone will. Even the groom. But it's not about the wedding details.

It's not really the napkin colors you're fighting about, even if those are the words coming out of your mouth. It's not about the mother of the bride's harsh manner, or the father of the bride's snobbery. It's not the place cards or the roses or whether or not the bride and groom will have a religious ceremony. And it's not what the others are accusing you of either. It's about fear. Fear of change. Fear of loss.

No, I haven't channeled Dr. Phil. I've just seen it thousands of times in my ten years of writing wedding books. I've seen mothers wreck their relationships with their daughters and sons by freaking out over the small stuff (like how many desserts there should be in addition to the cake) instead of just admitting, I'm scared here.

The sooner you admit your inner feelings about the big change that your son's wedding represents, the sooner you'll start to think, journal, or talk out your fears and concerns about "losing" your son, becoming a mother-in-law, feeling like you're "old" or have been replaced in some way. . . . Once you tackle your inner fears, the sooner the bride and groom get *you* back, minus the Spell, and the sooner you can get back into planning the wedding as a happy and supportive planning partner.

I Get It . . . They Don't

You might "get it" and have your priorities in line, your fears taken care of, but that doesn't mean that everyone else does. In your enlightened state, you can see right through the mother of the bride's bad attitude. She's scared. You can see why the bride is being crabby. Inside, she's terrified. And you can see why your son is popping Tums left and right: he's scared because of how scared the bride is.

In your clarity you can see it. But what can you do about it without being branded a know-it-all? Remember, the others may not want to be analyzed and "healed." Spouting psychology to them could well be the wrong thing to do. So do the one thing you can do. Be the one person who doesn't make the bride and groom crazy. Be the one who listens. You won't believe how correct a choice that will be in this situation.

When you have to deal with a steamroller mom or a stepmother who's switched her bossiness to high gear, defer where you can, choose your battles wisely, and keep your own boundaries and moral values. Don't get sucked into a power struggle. Rather, steer the conversation back to the bride and groom's wishes and happiness. Lead by example; be the dove of peace. The couple will thank you later.

The Number-One Mistake the Mother of the Groom Can Make

The biggest mistake even the wisest moms make when faced with a tough planning team is gossiping. Whether to the bride or to other family members and friends, complaining about what "a difficult person" the mother of the bride is will only add fuel to the flames of your quickly growing problem. Sure, it's healthy to vent, but vent to an uninvolved third party if you have to, not to another major player in the wedding plans . . . and definitely not to your son. Putting him in the middle and stressing him out when he wants you to get along with his bride's family will only hurt him.

You Are Not Alone

Remember, if there's a wedding coordinator involved, you have the invaluable aid of a professional who has dealt with much more problematic players. Ask the coordinator for advice on handling the situation. Coordinators are trained and experienced in facilitating cooperation and the goals of the bride and groom. Ask for help managing that out-of-control stepmother. Depend on the coordinator to help solve the problem.

In the religious realm, some brides and grooms have gone so far as to bring all of their parents into a counseling session with their officiant(s) of choice. Some brides and grooms experience intense friction with their parents and grandparents over how or if they'll include religion in their weddings. (Ask yourself now, Is this our situation?) Some parents and grandparents get irate if they think their own

Quick Comebacks

When another player comes to you with a criticism of your ideas, or you hear of some behind-the-back strategy intended to change an already-set decision, here are some quick comebacks to avoid trouble:

- "It's unfortunate that you don't agree with the decision, but this is how the bride instructed me to do it."
- "It would be a big mistake to try to get me to change a decision made by the bride and groom."
- "Wow, sometimes you surprise me." (And leave it at that.)
- "It's not about what we want. It's about what the kids want. I'm going to respect that."
- "Sure, I'll ask the bride and groom if they want it that way. I'm going to be speaking with them this evening." (This one stuns a true game-player who underestimated you.)

faith isn't being given its due or if religion won't be sufficiently emphasized in the proceedings. Bride and groom, frustrated, hope the priest or rabbi can help. And again, often, he can by explaining the couple's wishes in a voice of authority, and also by helping the entire group to find compromises that will make everyone happy.

In the most challenging situations, where the best of your efforts don't seem to be working, sometimes it's best to ask for professional help.

When It's the Bride You Can't Deal With

I've been pretty tough on the mother of the bride thus far, using her as an example of one of the most common sources of conflict for the mother of the groom. Less frequently—yet frequent enough to warrant a mention in this book—it is the bride who creates the biggest diplomatic problems for a mother of the groom.

You may adore your future daughter-in-law. She's already become part of the family and you love her like your own. If that's the case, then skip this section. You're one of the lucky ones.

Or . . . you could be in quite a difficult situation if your son is marrying a woman you don't like and never clicked with. She has an attitude. She's an elitist. She treats your son like her personal servant, and he's handed over his spine to her as he caters to her every whim. The kinds of complaints that moms have about the future bride are countless. She's from a different religious faith. You don't approve of her lifestyle. You think she's all about your son's money. The list goes on and on.

Not liking the bride is something you're going to have to deal with. Find a way to peacefully coexist for your son's sake. And look for some common ground. She is going to be your daughter-in-law, like it or not, and you run the risk of losing your son if you can't get a handle on your feelings toward her. As one mom told me, "you find a way to love her" even if she's not the person you'd pick for your son to marry. He's an adult and he makes his own choices. Except in extreme situations where you definitely should intervene with your son (e.g., she's a criminal), your job as Mom is to allow your son his choice.

That said, let's dive into the more common situation. You love your son's fiancée, but she's under the Spell. She's stressed out, difficult, snappy, and acting like a spoiled three-year-old. It's the Spell all right; she's in the web of fear. How do you work with someone who's in that web, someone who is not on her best behavior?

First, understand her. The poor woman is going through a lot with wedding stress, work stress, dealing with the prospect of becoming a wife, and also being pulled in many different directions by, say, her family and even the groom. With all those stressors, it's no wonder that she's not her best self right now.

That said, here are some dos and don'ts for dealing with her when she's a little out of control. Note that the don'ts may be more important than the dos, as it's extremely difficult to undo a faux pas that can change the course of your relationship with the bride and her family.

Do:

* Choose your moment to approach her. If you can see or hear that she's tired, busy, or upset, obviously now is not the time to dump your problems on her.

* Respect her time. Make an appointment to talk with her, especially during the day. If she's at work, she won't appreciate your calling her to talk wedding plans. Ask her when would be a good time for you to chat.

* Be patient when you leave messages for her. It may be your way to return calls or e-mails right away, but she might be so swamped that it will take her a few days to get back to you.

* Be a welcoming influence in her life. Be a pleasure to talk to and deal with.

* Diversify. Talk with her about other things besides the wedding, like current events, movies, and TV shows she likes. I can't emphasize enough that today's stressed brides want to be treated like the people they are and not just a bride-to-be.

* Keep it short. Be efficient. Let her know the issue at hand in a succinct e-mail or direct voice-mail message. The simpler your presentation of the problem or the update, the simpler it will be for her.

- Understand if she changes her mind about any of the wedding plans. It's her right.
- Cut the conversation short if she's in a bad mood. This is no time to accomplish anything successfully.

Don't:

- Criticize her or anything to do with the wedding. She doesn't need any more dissent.
- Put your son in the middle. If you have to deliver a message to the bride, e-mail or call her yourself. Grooms hate getting caught between their brides and their moms.
- Badmouth her family. You may not like them, and that's fine. But your son has to find a way to get along with them. Even if the bride is venting to you about her mom, don't be a co-conspirator. Brides dish about their mothers and then they forgive them. You won't be let off the hook so easily.
- Be helpless. Find the balancing point between getting the bride's okay and acting like you can't accomplish a simple task without assistance.
- Change who you are. The bride needs to get to know you, to grow closer to you.
- Lose sight of the fact that there will be a marriage for them after this wedding. When asked, you can come up with the greatest advice (e.g., "Sarah, this is actually a good challenge right now. It will help you and Paul figure out how to deal with others' input as a team, as a united front.")
- Start talking about kids yet. They have enough to worry about, so don't get ahead of them . . . even joking around.

From a Distance

Here's a common dilemma that's gaining prominence in these days of great distance between family members and friends. What if you live in one state, the bride and groom live in another state, and the bride's family lives in yet another? What if you're clear across the country from where the wedding will take place? Distance planning is a new challenge for wedding teams of today, which reminds us once again of the importance of communication. That's where e-mail and phone come in. It is possible to stay in touch and involved with the wedding plans via e-mail, so assure everyone that you can all work as if you're in the same place. With scanners and site links, faxes, and even one or two flights out to the wedding locale to scout and inspect, it can be done. Many couples tell me they budgeted in a flight or two to their parents' hometown, or even to a destination wedding site, for much-needed in-person experience and interviews. So be prepared to take a trip yourself! It's another good reason to visit your son and his bride, should the wedding be held near them. Yes, you have to be mobile, and it takes a bit of extra effort and expense, but consider it an investment in sharing this time with the couple. And stay in regular touch with them. Your participation is important, but if you show that you can overcome distance to help them, it will prove priceless.

CHAPTER 4

When Money Becomes an Issue

MONEY IS ALWAYS a major issue when you're planning a wedding. Weddings are expensive, with the average wedding budget across the country totaling between $25,000 and $50,000, depending on which survey you're looking at. Designer gowns can run up to five figures, and you can pay a per-guest fee of over $200 in some larger cities and big-budget regions. One centerpiece—just one, for one guest table—can cost $150. Yes, weddings are expensive, and there have been more than a few couples out there who have struggled between devoting that money to their wedding . . . or eloping and using that cash as a great downpayment on their new home.

The bride and groom know that their wedding dream comes with a price tag. And it may cause them some heartache. Some choose to plan smaller weddings and invite fewer of their loved ones. Some plan destination weddings for a great experience shared with only a dozen or so of their friends and family. Others cut their dream wedding to pieces, scaling down their hopes because they're worried about the expense and later regret the things they didn't have on that day.

Rest assured, money is a nearly universal concern . . . except for those brides and grooms with a golden checkbook. Their trust fund or a wealthy relative has taken the stress out of it for them. I've spoken to many parents of the bride who say that spending $150,000 on the wedding was worth it just to make their daughter happy. And some brides and grooms set their wedding date two to three years ahead, giving them time to save up to pay for the wedding they want.

"We didn't want to burden our parents with an expensive wedding." —Trey and Carla

"We wanted the wedding to be our way, and paying for it was the only way we'd have total control over it." —George and Sarah

"I saw how my mom was when my sister got married. She went absolutely nuts over all the details and didn't enjoy it at all. We didn't want that to happen again, so we saved for two years and paid for the wedding ourselves." —Lisa, bride

More and more couples are bucking tradition and taking on the financial burdens and thus the planning pressures and joys on their own. Their reasons for doing this are unique to each couple, but all of them can have pride in knowing they did it themselves and that money won't be a factor for their families.

Another growing trend is having both sets of parents contribute to the wedding fund. More parents = more checkbooks = more budget = more wedding. In a more benevolent sense, most couples tell me they're happy to share the planning with their families, so that they can be a part of creating something wonderful as well.

No matter where you are on the financial scale, which tax bracket you're in, and what kind of grand total you're working with, no matter if you're an equal planning partner or the couple has simply farmed out a few expenses to you, there's no escaping the subject of money. So now we have this . . . a group of emotionally charged wedding planning participants and the equally emotionally charged issue of money. Look out.

First, the Traditional Model

The first thing most couples and their families look for when they're about to approach the issue of who pays for what is the traditional model, the "rules" of which family gets to pay for each element of the wedding. Yes, the twenty-first-century wedding couples and their families break the rules. The bride's family no longer must pay for just about everything, and most wedding plans are personalized for each participant. Some couples nevertheless choose to stick with tradition. So here is the traditional list of who pays for what. Feel free to follow it, or break the rules.

What the Bride pays for:

* Groom's wedding ring
* Groom's wedding gift
* Bridal attendants' gifts
* Accommodations for out-of-town bridal party members
* After-the-wedding stationery

What the Groom pays for:

* Bride's engagement ring
* Bride's wedding ring
* Bride's wedding gift
* His own wedding day wardrobe
* Gifts for the male attendants
* Bride's bouquet
* Bride's going-away corsage or bouquet
* Corsages for the mothers and stepmothers, and perhaps grandmothers
* Boutonnieres for male bridal party members and fathers
* Marriage license
* Officiant's fee
* Honeymoon

What the Bride's Family pays for:

- Engagement party (if applicable)
- Wedding coordinator (if applicable)
- Ceremony cost: location, music, rentals, and all related expenses
- Entire cost of reception, including catering, wedding cake, beverages, entertainment, decor, rentals, and so on
- Bride's gown, veil, and all accessories
- Wedding gift
- Wedding invitations and announcements
- Postage for the invitations, announcements, and other mailed items
- Bouquets for the bridesmaids
- Transportation for bridal party
- Bridesmaids' luncheon
- Bridal brunch on morning of the wedding
- Photography
- Videography
- Floral décor
- Favors
- Special sentimental items: unity candle, toasting flutes, ring pillow, and so on.
- Their own wedding day wardrobe
- Taxes and tips

What the Groom's Family pays for:

- Rehearsal expenses
- Rehearsal dinner

- Wedding gift
- Their own wedding wardrobe
- Travel and lodging for groom's family members (optional)
- Special sentimental items: unity candle, toasting flutes, ring pillow, and so on
- Any general expenses they may wish to contribute
- Taxes and tips

What the Attendants pays for:

- Wedding wardrobe and accessories
- Fittings and alterations
- Their own travel and lodging expenses (if not complimentary)
- Wedding gift
- Shower
- Bachelor/bachelorette party

What the Bride and Groom pays for:

- Gifts for bridal party and parents
- Gifts for all who helped with the wedding
- Extra expenses not covered by the parents' budget
- Medical examinations and blood tests, as required

That's the traditional model, which the couple might wish to follow. At the end of this chapter, you'll find a worksheet where you'll record which elements you'll plan and pay for. It's an extension of the who's doing what worksheet from the previous chapter. I've separated them since the first checklist is about tasks and the second is just about what you're paying for. If you're just handing over the cash or picking up the tab for choices the bride and groom are making, this is where you record what's yours to pay for. Big difference, and it's smart to separate the two. So get ready to keep your financial contributions organized.

Opening the Money Box

Luckily, this is not your battle. It's up to the bride and groom to decide how to set their budget and how to include your family and the bride's family in it. Especially in cases where one family has much more money than the other, it can be a touchy topic for the bride and groom to handle without offending anyone. How do they discuss money with you all as a group? It's their job to broach that subject, but you can make it much easier on them by discussing or broaching any concerns *you* have about working with a family that has far more, or far less, than you do.

If you are asked for advice, you might be able to help the couple find a great solution. Here are some of the most popular and successful ways couples have opened up the money issue when finances could be a sticking point between their two families:

- When you all sit down to discuss financial contributions to the wedding, consider making it a blind donation system. That is, both families will hand over a check for the amount they wish to give to the cause, sealed in a plain envelope, with no mention of amounts enclosed. The bride and groom would then deposit the check into an account set up specifically for the wedding.

"My Dad is very Old World. Money is a big issue to him. He'd be offended if he knew what Anne's family was giving if it's more than what he could give, and then he'd give more than he can afford to 'beat' my fiancée's parents. Then, he'd resent them. I know how he is, how he gets. The blind donation system works to solve all that." —Jim, groom

* The bride and groom can openly discuss budgets for the areas of the wedding that are most important to them. In my books for brides, I encourage couples to start off planning their budget by making a priority list; that is, selecting the elements of their wedding to which they plan to devote larger portions of their budget. It might be that the bride wants a sea of flowers at the wedding, so she'll put a larger percentage of the money toward that and then less toward the invitations, for instance. With such a priority list in hand, they can then share their wishes either openly or in private conversations with each set of parents. Sometimes discretion is a better mode of conduct when sensitivities are likely to be more acute.

* Or parents can choose from individual tasks that the bride and groom have assigned dollar values to, rather than just rankings. Knowing the couple wants to spend $5,000 on flowers could be just the information you need to take that task, share it, or let the bride's family take care of it.

Where Will You Get the Money?

It's the same dilemma the bride and groom are in, or are at least concerned about: Where is this money coming from? With so few of us setting aside money for retirement and with the kids' college funds already tapped out and spent, how do you pull an extra $10,000 out of nowhere to be a full partner for that $30,000 wedding the kids want?

Mothers of grooms share what works and what doesn't:

> *"Set up a wedding fund when it looks like the bride and groom*
> *are heading to the chapel. With auto-deposits, you can accumulate*
> *a few thousand dollars to help out without hurting your balance*
> *on your credit cards too much." —Irene*

> *"Use your tax refund check." —Carla*

"Set an amount you're willing to put on your credit cards right now, and also right now create a payment plan for yourself to pay it back after the wedding."—Tara

And now for some don'ts:

"Don't take out a loan on your house." —Mariellen

"Don't max out your credit cards. You never know when an emergency will arise with one of your other kids, with medical expenses, and other major problems." —Tracy

"Don't sell valuable items. My friend sold her porcelain doll collection to be able to help pay for her son's expensive wedding, and while she loved being able to help give them a great day, she really hurt afterward being without her collection." —Eileen

"Don't ever, ever, ever borrow money from family or friends."
—Renata

And speaking of don'ts, here are a few more:

- Don't allow the money issue to ruin everything for the bride and groom. They should be focusing on the symbolism of the wedding, not sweating every bill. As a group, you'll find a way to give them the day they want.
- Don't load the emotional money issue by making a big deal out of it, by expecting any kind of praise for your generosity, or by apologizing for not being able to give more. Rise above the dollar amounts to focus on the importance of what you're helping to create.

* Don't rip yourself off. Find creative ways to get more wedding for less money. Every big-ticket item can be found for a lot less than you think. All it takes is a bit of extra time, some creativity, and a little luck.

Work Your Network

The smartest wedding teams check their personal networks of friends, family, and colleagues to see if anyone can "help out" with the wedding. No, not by soliciting cash from them, but rather seeing if anyone can get you a break or a freebie in their industry as their wedding gift to the couple; for instance, an uncle who works for a limousine company might be able to wrangle a nice, big discount on stretch limos for the couple . . . or arrange to have the second limousine provided for free. By calling in a favor that uncle has contributed a priceless part of the wedding day, and he now doesn't have to go out and get a gift.

Through sheer luck, my parents happened to have gone to high school with a local restaurateur, who gave us a 50 percent discount on the per-guest charges . . . which amounted to a big break on the total cost of my wedding.

Here are some stories from couples who used the "networking discount" to their advantage:

> *"My aunt owns a beach house overlooking the ocean, and as her wedding gift to us, we got to use it as the location for our wedding! We saved thousands, and she got to show off her home to the entire family."* —Erin and Tad

> *"Our friend works at a winery, so we were able to have our wedding there for a big discount."* —Nancy and Thomas

You get the idea. Here's a place to note down any people you know who might be able to provide the networking discount:

* _____

* _____

❧ _____

❧ _____

❧ _____

❧ _____

The Barter System

If you don't have a close relative with a beach house or an "in" at the Four Seasons, there's always the barter system.

You would trade three hours of your accounting skills in exchange for your friend the pastry chef's expertise in making petit fours for the rehearsal dinner. You could trade four hours of baby-sitting for your friend the musician's one hour of playing the harp at the cocktail hour.

Check with friends, and friends of friends, your own supportive circles, to see if bartering is the way to go. I heard from one couple who was amazed at the groom's mother's ability to wheel and deal with bartering. At last count, the mother had bartered the design of personalized Web sites for business owners ("It takes me no time at all, really . . . it's easy") to get borrowed potted plants for the reception ("They'll go back after the wedding"), the wedding cake and groom's cake ("I did a major site for them, and they gave me $2,000 worth of cake for free!"), free alterations for the bride's gown and her gown, and a big discount on the favors ("An artist friend was just starting her own homemade favors company, so I hooked her up with her own Web site to get her started"). Not bad. She's giving her time and talents to others, helping them launch or expand their businesses, and she's also helping to give the bride and groom a wedding they wouldn't otherwise be able to afford.

Now, it's your turn. What can you offer in exchange for others' services? List your particular talents or sideline abilities here:

❧ _____

❧ _____

* _____

* _____

* _____

* _____

Using Your Rewards

What about using the rewards points on your credit card to get some services or items for free? Great idea. Why not cash in the points or frequent flier miles you've earned to help the bride and groom? Even better, as it's smart to use credit cards to protect the purchases you'll make for the wedding, you can earn even more points from your wedding purchases. Some parents tell me they either cashed in their points to give the bride and groom some freebies for the honey-

---

Anybody Want a Baby-sitter?

So where do you go to network for bartering possibilities? Some cities have established bartering clubs. Check with the town's chamber of commerce or the town library. If one doesn't already exist, you can always be a trailblazer and start a community bartering club. If you don't want to go that far, then start talking to everyone in your circle of friends, put up fliers at the library and in coffee shops ("Looking for a talented pianist in exchange for personal Web site design services"), and talk to people in your book club, the PTA, alumni clubs, and so on. Spread the word, and the bartering system you need right now could bring you just the kind of contact you're looking for.

---

moon, or they used their points to get gift certificates they could use for wedding favors, guest books, and even great outfits for the rehearsal dinner and bridal brunch. Using rewards points or miles can be quite a perk when you're helping to pay for an expensive wedding.

Check out the rates and fine print for any reward card you're using, and dig out those pamphlets that came with your card. They will tell you about partner sponsor benefits, such as getting double points for shopping at stores that are in a special program with the credit card company. Be safe and smart about your use of credit, and cash in for some nice rewards.

Wedding Budget Worksheet

Here's a wedding budget worksheet. Keep it flexible as you go through the process. Some purchases will cost more or less than you originally figured, and then there's always the surprise of getting items or services for free. So use pencil while you're filling in the figures, and use this chart to keep you on track.

ITEM/SERVICE	WHO'S PAYING	BUDGETED	ACTUAL
Engagement announcement cards			
Newspaper engagement announcement			
Engagement party			
Ceremony site			
Ceremony décor			
Officiant's fee			
Marriage license			
Blood tests			

ITEM/SERVICE	WHO'S PAYING	BUDGETED	ACTUAL
Pre-wedding counseling/classes			
Reception-site booking			
Décor for reception site			
Rentals for reception site (tents, linens, tables, and so on)			
Preparation of reception site (landscaping, cleaning, and so on)			
Charges for delivery, setup, and cleanup of reception site			
Additional permits for parking and so on			
Wedding gown			
Wedding gown fittings and alterations			
Accessories and shoes			
Bride's manicure, pedicure, and hair			
Groom's clothing			
Groom's accessories			
Groom's manicure, pedicure, and other treatments			
Wedding coordinator			
Invitations			
Postage			
Programs			
Thank-you notes			

ITEM/SERVICE	WHO'S PAYING	BUDGETED	ACTUAL
Save-the-date cards			
Place cards			
Menu cards			
Caterer's menu			
Liquor and beverages			
Cake			
Additional desserts			
Bouquets			
Corsages			
Boutonnieres			
Floral centerpieces and other floral décor			
Cocktail party entertainment			
Reception entertainment			
Photography			
Videography			
Wedding cameras			
Limousines or classic cars			
Other guest transportation			
Guest lodging			
Guest gift baskets			
Wedding weekend activity #1			
Wedding weekend activity #2			
Wedding weekend activity #3			

ITEM/SERVICE	WHO'S PAYING	BUDGETED	ACTUAL
Favors _____			
Gifts _____			
Toss-its _____			
Shower party expenses (optional) ___			
Shower gifts _____			
Wedding night lodging for bride and groom _____			
Honeymoon travel expenses _____			
Honeymoon accommodations _____			
Tips _____			
Totals _____			

PART TWO

Getting Into the Details: The Ceremony and Wedding Day Plans

CHAPTER 5

So, Have You Set a Date Yet?

So, HAVE YOU set a date yet?

That's the number-one question everyone is asking the bride and groom—and probably you, too—right now. After all, the date of the wedding determines just about everything *about* the wedding itself—the style, the location (as in, Will it be outdoors in late summer?), the budget. As you might already know, weddings are much cheaper at some times of the year than others.

No other plans can be made until the date is set. In this section, you'll learn about the stylistic and strategic benefits of the day, month, even year of the wedding. What seems like only a square on the calendar dictates everything you'll do from here on in. So let's start looking at timing details for the big day.

How Much Time 'Til Then?

When you're looking at a massive planning job, not to mention the fact that most of the great locations and experts are already booked by other engaged couples a year or two before the wedding, you can never have too much time to plan. That's why so many couples set their wedding date at least a year ahead. Fourteen months is the average "waiting time" or planning period, during which most couples have the needed time to research their wedding experts, book them, and orchestrate the many hundreds of other wedding details while still running their lives, careers, social obligations, and so on. The more time they allow, the better. So much for instant gratification!

Of course, it is certainly possible to plan a wedding in less than a year's time, with an organized approach, lots of help, and perhaps a little bit of luck. One of my most popular books is *How to Plan an Elegant Wedding in 6 Months or Less*. It can be done, and done well, and plenty of couples are getting to the altar more quickly.

The choice is up to the couple. They're aware of their own time constraints and the amount of work needed to achieve their dream wedding. If they're planning to save money to pay for their wedding, that's also an understandable reason for a far-off wedding date.

So don't be surprised if you find out the wedding will take place two years from now, perhaps even three. That's just more time you all have to plan the wedding at a comfortable pace, and enjoy it every step along the way. Good things come to those who can patiently wait.

The Season for a Reason

"We wanted our wedding to take place during the autumn months, when the leaves on all the trees would be bright orange and yellow and burgundy. It made for gorgeous scenery at our outdoor wedding— no extra floral décor needed—and our pictures came out beautifully!" —Tamara and Rob

Tamara and Rob got it right. Hold your wedding during the most beautiful season of the year—your favorite, whatever season that may be—and enjoy the perks of nature as a benefit. If it's a summertime outdoor wedding the couple craves, then you know which months to look at in your region. To help determine the season of the wedding, here are some pros and cons for each. Feel free to add your own to the lists:

Summer

Pros

- Gorgeous weather
- Ideal for an outdoor wedding, including beach weddings
- Ideal for additional wedding-weekend activities
- Guests' kids are out of school, making it easier to attend wedding
- _____

Cons

- Dog-day weather with temperatures hitting uncomfortable highs
- Possible summertime rainstorms and hurricanes
- Peak travel and tourism times could make expenses higher for you and your guests
- Peak wedding season means availabilities could be lower and prices higher
- Summer events in the family, such as graduation parties, can compete with the wedding event
- As one bride reported, "I forgot all about allergy season!"
- _____

Autumn

Pros

- Gorgeous outdoor scenery with fall foliage
- Fall décor items are available for far less than summer flowers
- Better wedding prices in the latter part of fall
- Travel companies may offer great rates for post-summer vacation fares

* Family gathers for the late-fall holiday of Thanksgiving, which could be the perfect time of year to have the wedding. After all, everyone might be in the area in this high-travel season.

* _____

Cons

* Nature doesn't change according to schedule—the leaves on the trees could fall more quickly than anticipated, and bad weather is always a possibility

* The kids go back to school, fall sports activities start, kids have sporting events they must attend on weekends, and some guests might not be able to make the wedding due to their kids' schedules

* Fall is quickly becoming one of the most popular seasons for weddings, so places and professionals might be booked up

* _____

Winter

Pros

* Gorgeous natural scenery . . . a landscape blanketed with pristine snow, trees crystallized with ice and sparkling in the sun, a frozen-over pond in the distance with ice skaters twirling and circling

* Holiday décor already in place everywhere you look, including poinsettias already placed inside churches, and streets and houses decorated for the holidays with strings of lights

* Plenty of holiday events planned in the area, making for wonderful wedding-weekend activities

* Sledding and ice-skating nearby are ideal wedding-weekend activities as well

* Kids and college students may be on their winter breaks from school

- Winter weddings are gaining in popularity, but not on the high-budget peak-season calendar . . . so prices might be lower in the wedding industry
- In the right conditions, outdoor wedding photos can be extra-creative and fun
- New Year's Eve . . . perfect for weddings!

- _____

Cons

- Harsh winter weather, snowstorms, and resulting traffic delays can make for wedding nightmares
- Peak travel season for the holidays will likely mean more expensive fares for those traveling
- Family holiday commitments might make it hard for guests to attend the wedding, especially if they'd have to travel
- Having photos taken outdoors could be iffy when weather is bad

- _____

Spring

Pros

- Gorgeous weather, beautiful scenery
- The availability of spring flowers, which can be less expensive than ordering wedding flowers during other seasons
- Symbolism of new beginnings, new growth, plants starting to bloom
- Spring is ideal for weddings, taking place just before the peak season with its higher prices

- _____

Cons

- ✤ Unpredictable spring weather, including lots of rain and perhaps unseasonably cold days

- ✤ Allergy season is at its peak now, and for some the sneezing and watery eyes can be quite unpleasant

- ✤ _____

Of course, there are many more pros and cons that might occur to you regarding the seasons. Your area of the country might be mild in winter, or mild year-round, so the weather issue won't concern you. Your family might have its own seasonal issues, like the busy tax season if you're all accountants, or the holiday sales season if you own a store. Consider seasonal pros and cons specific to you, your specific limits and assure the bride and groom that they can overcome any seasonal setback that arises with forethought and good planning (perhaps some rentals) . . . so they should choose the season they love most.

The Ideal Month

Years ago, May and June were the most popular months for weddings. That tradition hearkens back to the ancient days when the months of May and June were times of early harvest in villages, and the abundance of the new harvest lent itself to wedding celebrations. Now, peak wedding months have much to do with the weather. May through October are the peak wedding months of this century, bringing with them higher prices due to supply and demand, people's more open summer travel and vacation schedules, and also a very-booked world of wedding professionals and locations, as mentioned earlier. Peak wedding season is either a time to be avoided or embraced, according to your particular budget and timing requirements.

However, don't make the mistake of thinking that a January wedding will always be less expensive and easier to plan than a June wedding. Any wedding at any time can acheive monstrous proportions and resultant enormous costs. Every wedding plan is shaped by the individual decisions made by the planner. While

It's Raining, It's Pouring . . .

What if it rains on the wedding day? That's unfortunately something you can't prevent by sheer will alone. Rain has caused countless moves of wedding locations and photo-shoot settings, and it has caused many a bride's tears to fall as well. It might ring hollow to the bride, but you can try to cheer her a little if you let her know that rain falling on the wedding day is considered in many cultures to be a sign of good fortune for the couple. Here are some other cultural superstitions about wedding day weather:

- Rain on the wedding day means fertility for the couple, and many children.
- A rainbow after a quick rainstorm means the couple will always prosper after the challenges that arise in their marriage.
- Snow falling on the wedding day leads to financial gain in the marriage.
- A mighty storm with lots of rain, snow, or wind isn't so positive. It is said to predict a stormy marriage—so just hand her a glass of champagne and keep the superstitions to yourself.

you'll surely find lower prices in the off-seasons, the difference usually influences only a portion of the budget. Great buys can be found in any month of the year, so don't limit yourselves to snowstorm or hurricane season just because you think it will be cheaper. With the exception of Super Bowl Sunday, every day of the year offers unique advantages for weddings.

Holidays: Love Them or Leave Them Alone?

A recent survey says that Super Bowl Sunday, the day of the biggest pro-football game of the year, is the *least* popular day for weddings. Couples who inadvertently chose this particular Sunday wound up with guests who crowded the bar area to watch the game on TV rather than dance to the deejay's music or watch the cutting of the cake. Some guests even brought mini-TVs into the reception hall to watch at their tables, erupting in cheers at every touchdown or interception. And it's not just the men choosing the game over the wedding . . . women are big football fans too.

Why all this fuss over Super Bowl Sunday? It's one example of the bad side of choosing a holiday or holiday weekend as the date of the wedding.

Of course, there are good points to having weddings on holidays. New Year's Eve is popular for weddings. Consider the festivities, the family and friends who are all together on the biggest party night of the year, and the exciting countdown to midnight. Celebrities and regular people often check first to see if New Year's Eve is available for their weddings.

Valentine's Day, too, is another popular choice for a holiday wedding. Romance, sentiment, slow dancing, an anniversary the groom can't possibly forget . . . V-Day is a top choice.

Thanksgiving weekend, when the family is all together. Perfect for a wedding.

The week *after* Christmas or Hanukkah (never before; people are just too frantic with shopping and travel plans), are also popular choices for weddings.

Memorial Day Weekend and Labor Day Weekend give you a three- to five-day weekend for guests' travel, wedding-weekend activities, and lots of time to enjoy the summer events in the area.

What's the downside to holiday-weekend weddings? Travel and expense. It might be a lot to ask guests to forego their family vacation plans or to hit the highways along with everyone else on these big holiday travel weekends. Also, in the world of weddings, wedding professionals know these weekends are popular, so they're likely to hike their prices. During peak vacation times, hotels will charge higher rates. There's always an up and down side to holiday-weekend plans, so consider your guests' needs and service availabilities before making the final decision.

Save the Date

If the bride and groom choose a holiday weekend or even peak wedding season in the summer months, or a destination wedding where travel will be required, be sure to send out Save-the-Date cards announcing the couple's wedding date and location at least six months in advance. This is a smart move that gives guests a chance to plan their travel and to clear their schedules so they can attend the wedding.

Destination Weddings

Check out the ideal months for weddings planned in faraway lands or tropical islands, the locales of choice for the popular destination weddings of today. It may be snowing in your hometown in January, but it's 80 degrees in Puerto Rico. So talk to an accredited travel agent to find out the likely weather and travel conditions for the destinations the couple has in mind. Find out when that location's tropical storm season is, when the bug season is, when it's *not* tourism season and therefore many of the local attractions will be closed. (You'd be surprised at the number of destination weddings deflated by out-of-season disappointments like these!) A bit of research with a travel professional can help the couple choose the best location at the right time of year for the getaway wedding of a lifetime.

Saturday, Sunday . . . Thursday?

Obviously, the most common day for weddings is Saturday, but an increasing number of couples have discovered a now not-so-hidden secret about getting more wedding for their money: avoiding the Saturday-night wedding and choosing a different day of the week. Friday night is the big one, with many couples having an identical, formal wedding as the couple who booked the Saturday-night time slot, but for *15–20 percent less*. The hotel/restaurant/banquet hall gets another wedding that weekend, so they can charge a little less.

Sunday afternoon is growing in popularity for formal weddings or formal luncheons, brunches and cocktail parties—and even the earlier time slot of noon on Saturday is picking up steam. Your party ends at 4 P.M., and the next party rolls in at 5 P.M. It's brilliant planning on the hotel's part, and equally smart planning for couples who choose the earlier time on Saturday. Some couples say their guests drink less at the earlier Saturday reception, which turns out to be safer and less expensive all around.

Now here's a creative option for even bigger savings: a Thursday-night wedding, which is ideal if most guests live close to the reception site. I've seen Thursday-night formal receptions priced at 25 percent less than their weekend counterparts, so check it out.

Small, intimate wedding celebrations are now held in the afternoons on weekends, or in the evenings on weekday nights, proving once again that any day has its advantages for weddings, depending on your circumstances. It's a whole new world when it comes to choosing the day of the week and time.

Time of Day

Now here is where things *haven't* changed and aren't even likely to. With few exceptions, the time of day chosen for the wedding still dictates the degree of formality. Check out the chart here to determine this part of the wedding plans:

It's About Time!

Type of Reception	Time of Day (Start Time)
Brunch	11 A.M.–1 P.M.
Luncheon	noon–2 P.M.
Tea	3 P.M.–4 P.M.
Cocktail Party	4 P.M.–7 P.M.

Dinner	5 P.M.–8 P.M.
Champagne and Dessert	8 P.M.–10 P.M.
Late Night	9 P.M.–midnight

Dinner-hour weddings usually are formal, or ultraformal, often black tie or white tie. A cocktail party may be formal or semiformal. The others might be less formal, depending on the couple's wishes for their wedding. For an outdoor afternoon wedding, you can go formal with the full treatment . . . or less formal as in a laid-back beach wedding with a barefoot bride and guests in sundresses or khaki pants and white shirts. Those choices are up to you, guided, of course, by the rules of timing for the wedding's formality. Style is an element that will help you all make the right plans for the right time of day.

When Ties and Tails Are Too Much

The formality of the wedding can be an area of conflict among brides and grooms, their parents, and other planners. The couple might prefer casual. They might not want the ultraformal event of the season that you're dreaming of, with all guests in formalwear, a full orchestra, champagne, and caviar. Remember, their dream might not always match your dream.

I've heard many wedding-planning teams start arguing because the groom doesn't want a "royal wedding" while everyone else is imagining him in white tie and tails. Or the bride wants a more relaxed wedding celebration where everyone can be comfortable.

Here's an ideal compromise: the wedding reception itself can be formal, or ultraformal, and then the *after-party* can be less formal. That's right . . . there's often an after-party for which the couple and their guests might change into more comfortable attire, relax in a quieter setting, and just spend time with loved ones. Knowing this more laid-back, late-into-the-night gathering is coming after the reception might be enough to get the couple to agree to spend a portion of the day in formal mode.

And remember, there will be many wedding-weekend activities. For the happiness of all, plan some that are formal and some that are casual. It would be a

Sunrise, Sunset

One aspect of timing the wedding might be the bride and groom's wishes to have the ceremony take place at sunset on the beach or with a beautiful mountain backdrop. It might be a wish for great ambiance, or a spiritual moment, or just the knowledge that sunset would make for great pictures, but couples love the sunset. So you can help them out by researching on the *Old Farmer's Almanac* online site (www.almanac.com) for the exact time of sunset (and sunrise, should that be their wish) for any day of the year. The Navy's Web site (www.usno.navy.mil) also includes a sunrise and sunset tracker in their naval observatory reports.

drain if everyone had to dress up in their best for every event. Throw in a relaxed, casual gathering where you can.

What you'll find as you get into the beginning of the wedding plans is that setting the date for the wedding is dependent upon finding the *locations* for the ceremony and reception—which we'll get into in the next chapter. Most often, it's the tricky coordinating of an available ceremony site and an available reception site that really determines the day of the wedding. Thousands of couples out there book early, so you're about to find out the logistics of coordinating the place and the time.

Once you get these foundations set, you can go on to help plan the entirety of the wedding from start to finish as you look forward to the big day!

CHAPTER 6

Location Scouting

BEAUTIFUL WEDDINGS take place in gorgeous settings . . . a grand cathedral with high, vaulted ceilings, polished oak pews, magnificent stained-glass windows; a grand and elegant synagogue; a lush lawn of an historic estate home with gardens and cobblestone paths; a fine-sand beach with a limitless view of the horizon as the sun sets. The perfect wedding calls for the perfect location, and here is where you'll start your search for the perfect setting for ceremony and reception alike.

As mentioned earlier, very often it takes finding available days and times at the most-wished-for locations, then coordinating between the ceremony and reception locations' openings before the actual wedding date can be set. That technicality aside, it's all about finding sites with all the beauty you want as well as a few functional aspects (Is it big enough to fit the number of guests?) to make that the perfect spot for the wedding day.

Before you go any further, make sure you know what the bride and groom are thinking. They might already know exactly where they want to marry and where they want to celebrate. Brides of today might be modern women, but many still hold romantic notions of where their weddings will be. Ask first, and listen for answers such as "I want a beach wedding," "I want to marry at the church I have attended for years," "I want our reception to be at the Crystal Ballroom." The choice might already be made. But if it isn't. . . .

The Ceremony Site

In many cases, this isn't even a question. The couple is set on marrying at the church they attend or that their family has attended since they were children. There's not a doubt in their minds. That's the easy scenario.

But sometimes it's not that easy. . . .

Let's say, for instance, that *you* want them to marry in the church or synagogue that you attend. You believe that marriage is a holy act, and it should be set within the walls of a house of worship. Period. What would you think if the couple didn't want to marry there? That they want to marry in a field of flowers, or by a waterfall, or in a hotel ballroom with the mayor running the show? Your answer might be, Fine with me, but you need to know that the biggest powder keg in wedding planning is when the parents are *not* so open-minded. Full-scale battles can erupt when the couple wishes to marry outside of a house of worship.

Please don't be one of those parents who ruins everything and wrecks their relationship with their children over the choice of ceremony style and location. Be open to what the couple wants. Once again: It's their wedding, so whatever they want is what matters most.

Now, if the couple wishes to have a religious wedding, but they don't belong to a house of worship, or they will be coming back to your hometown to marry so they can't marry in the house of worship where they live, then it's time to do some holy-site shopping. Many churches and synagogues have strict rules about marrying people who don't belong to their organizations. I've heard from many couples who practically got the door slammed in their faces because the priest or rabbi said they had to be members (read: *paying* members). One bride was rejected from the church where she taught Bible School classes because she wasn't a registered parishioner! I'm warning you now so you won't be surprised about any religious-site red tape you may encounter.

Of course, there are far more houses of worship that embody what true faith should be: They welcome anyone and everyone who comes to them. These are the true gems out there, the ones that are waiting when others close the door in your face. Seek them out.

When it comes to choosing a house of worship, know that it's not just the interior decorating of any church or synagogue that matters, but how the bride and groom feel in the space. It's how the resident officiant speaks to them, how open he or she is to the couple's ideas, how welcomed they are. When the bride and groom walk into a house of worship that is "them," they know it. And the plans can go on from there.

A Bit of Paperwork and a Talk

Before anyone can marry in a house of worship, they'll need to speak with the officiant, schedule some counseling sessions, and discuss the ceremony plans. And they will also have to submit some paperwork. If one or both have been married before, they'll have to submit proofs of annulment, divorce papers, or even a certificate of death for a departed previous spouse. Some houses require proof of baptism or conversion. This paper chase is a way that religious houses keep track of who is being married and make sure their "clients" observe and respect their rules. It's a solid system of keeping the legitimacy in the marriages they perform, and they also believe strongly in guiding the couple toward the right questions and discussions about marriage and the future. It's a holy cause the couple should be prepared for.

"We Want a Religious Wedding, but Not in a House of Worship"

Sometimes a couple wants to respect the values of their faith—or faiths—but they do not wish to marry within the walls of a house of worship. With the consent of willing officiants, their plan is to marry in a secular place with the rites led by recognized religious leaders. This might also translate into a spiritual ceremony, as opposed to a religious one, with a trained officiant leading the very personalized service.

If this is the case, then you're free to scout any location for the wedding, from a hotel ballroom set up to accommodate the seating and the altar or chuppah you desire to an oceanside locale, a field of flowers, or your own backyard.

Alternative Locations

Today's couples who wish to venture outside of traditional wedding settings are looking at the following types of unique locations for their ceremonies, and often for their receptions as well:

- Beaches
- Backyards—the family home
- Backyards—the home of a friend or relative, as their gift to the couple
- Estate homes rented for the day
- Wineries
- Arboretums
- Family farms with tree groves and gazebos, open for rental
- Scenic overlooks
- County and state park areas
- Township gazebos
- Museums
- Art galleries
- Lighthouses
- Tourist attractions, such as Sea World and Disney World
- Alumni clubhouses
- University grounds
- Country clubs
- Restaurants with great views and private party rooms
- Marina clubhouses
- Yachts
- Beach houses with ocean views and great architecture
- Ski lodges

- Private villas overseas or on an island
- Zoos and wildlife reserves

The possibilities are endless. Some couples will marry on the grounds of a resort, while some are happy to float off in a hot-air balloon with their officiant, exchanging vows in midflight and then landing in a field where all their guests await with champagne glasses in hand and a five-star catered menu waiting for them under a tent.

The world of weddings means there's nothing that can't be done—well, almost. The bounds of creativity are expanding, and truly unique ceremonies and receptions can be found at every turn, in the most unexpected locations. So invest plenty of time in researching and visiting a wide range of locales.

Reception Location Extras

Of course, the reception sites you search will offer similar perks: a beautiful ball-room, a separate party room where the cocktail hour can be held, and great views and décor. But you should know that many new hotels, resorts, banquet facilities, and even restaurants have come up with brand-new attractions for the bride and groom's wedding dreams. Here are just some of the offerings you may find at the sites near you:

- A couples' lounge where the bride and groom can spend some pre-cocktail-party time alone or with their bridal parties. These rooms are decorated in style, with leather chairs, fireplaces, terrific views, terraces overlooking the ocean or a golf course, and VIP service from the staff.

- A *third* location for the guests to move to either for the cake cutting and dessert hour or for the after-party. This might be an elegant lounge or cigar bar with smoky jazz played on the sound system and cozy couches available for guest seating.

- Unique party settings at poolside. Forget the floating candles in the pool. Today's resorts are borrowing from the trendiest wedding coordinators and setting up bistro tables and couches at poolside, using special-effect lighting to project images onto the pool surface (even the bride and groom's names!), separate menus, and theme drinks.

* Separate bars by the reception location, such as a piano bar or a kids' lounge for under-13s. Wedding guests are free to roam the premises to find a spot that suits them, being sure to return in time for the cake cutting.

These are just *some* of the new attractions you'll find when you start looking at reception locations' special offerings. Prepare to be surprised by many more, especially when you're looking at exciting destination wedding locations.

Destination Locations

By *destination* I'm not always implying that you'll be jetting off to an island or to Disneyworld. The newest trend in destination weddings is traveling an hour or two from home to a nearby resort area, such as a beach region or ski lodge in the mountains, just a short hop from home. I recently scouted out some ski resorts *in the summertime* and found a world of wedding packages that brought with them incredible mild-weather perks: the best golf courses in the state, spa packages, family resorts that can be reserved for just your group of guests, horseback riding, hayrides, bicycle tours of wineries, and antique shops by the mile. All available for wedding groups . . . no plane flight or extensive (and expensive) travel necessary.

Couples who looked at these sites remarked that they were happy to bring their guests "away from it all" yet not burden them with the time and price of a long trip. It was just the getaway they had in mind, surprisingly close to home. So don't forget to look nearby for what could be the ideal wedding location.

If you are planning to go the distance—to a tropical island—check into all of the extra location perks you might find there as well . . . from special suites to oceanfront bungalows, family events and kids' activities, adventure sports, several restaurants on the resort grounds, places for pre-wedding cocktail parties. A friend who married on the island of Nevis said he and his bride reserved a local sugar mill for their rehearsal dinner—it was a unique location with great trees and flowers around it—and then they used the resort's elegant library for their post-reception gathering. All it took was some research into additional sites on or nearby the resort's grounds to uncover the most unique available spots. If you're working with an on-site wedding coordinator for a faraway destination wedding, be sure to ask about any interesting settings you might be able to weave into the wedding plans. Last-minute changes are always possible:

"Once we arrived at the island resort, we took part of the afternoon to go exploring. We discovered a horseshoe-shaped cove surrounded by cliffs, accessible by a pretty sand path with hibiscus flowers growing along it. We hadn't seen that setting in the brochures or on the Web site, so we asked our wedding coordinator if we could switch our ceremony site to that area instead of by the pool, as we'd originally booked. She made a few phone calls, and that site was ours!" —Sandra and Nick

Questions to Ask About Any Location

Be sure that the site being considered for the ceremony fits what you *need*, not just what you like. Of course, the place must be attractive and well kept, the personification of the bride and groom's dreams, but it also must be functional for the big day. So keep these criteria in mind when you're doing a walk-through of any location. (Always do a walk-through. Don't just choose a site from photos or a Web site! You'd be surprised at the number of couples who have wound up marrying at a lovely marina that's right next to a noisy airport, with low-flying planes that scare the life out of the guests. But it looked so pretty in the pictures!)

* Is the site large enough for our guest list?

* Is it too large for our guest list? (A cavernous site will look empty if you only have a handful of guests.)

* Are we allowed to set up a tent on the grounds? (Very important. Some sites say no, since they don't want tent holes in their lawns. Not finding this out soon enough can cause big problems.)

* Can we bring in our own rentals?

* Will this wedding be the only wedding taking place at this location on the big day? (Very important, since you don't want confusion at the site, or for the other couple to accidentally get your son's wedding cake. It has happened!)

* Will this wedding be the only *event* taking place at this location on the big day?

* If there will be an event at this location earlier in the day, how much time does the site allow for cleanup of that party and setup of yours?

* How early can the wedding professionals gain access to the site to set up for the wedding? (Make sure there's enough time.)

* Consider the privacy factor. Will you be shielded from public areas? Will onlookers be able to wander past the wedding?

* Will you need additional permits? Some sites require alcohol permits, parking permits, and exemptions from local noise curfews.

* How is the parking? Is there plenty of space or will you need to make arrangements at a local parking lot?

* How is the sound? In an outdoor site or a large indoor site you might need to wire the place with microphones and speakers so that guests can hear the vows.

* Is there power at the site, so that your experts can plug in their equipment? Or will you have to bring that in as well?

* How is the temperature? Always choose a space that offers air-conditioning or heat, depending on the season of the wedding. If not, will you have to rent and bring in heaters or air conditioners?

* Are there restrooms? Are they in good working order?

* Is there room for a separate baby-sitting area?

* Is there a coat check?

* In the case of holding the reception at the same area, is there a separate area where the caterer can make preparations?

* Is the place handicapped accessible or easily accessible by elderly guests? Sites with cobblestone paths or circular staircase entrances pose a challenge to some guests.

Of course, scout the sites on your list keeping function in mind, and get everyone thinking about possible snags or challenges to your party's unique requirements.

CHAPTER 7

Planning the Ceremony

CREATING THE CEREMONY—choosing religious readings and music, writing vows and the like—is up to the bride and groom, led by their officiant. Together, they'll decide which words, songs, and personalized touches speak their hearts and comprise this truly most important part of the wedding day, the reason for all the celebration to follow.

They may come to you for advice, perhaps for guidance on faith, décor ideas for the ceremony site, and even to "borrow" the readings and elements of your own wedding ceremony. You might contribute the perfect suggestions and advice to alleviate their concerns, you might be able to answer their biggest questions about what they want for their ceremony. A mother's advice is always valuable, and almost always kept in mind.

Overall, it's a very high priority for brides and grooms to include and honor their parents during the ceremony, and mothers especially are often invited to play a vital role in some of the most sentimental and symbolic rituals of the marriage service. Looking back in time, and also speaking to many interfaith, spiritual wedding officiants, I've discovered enormous ties between the rituals of marriage and the maternal influence. While it has traditionally been the father's role to "give the bride away" in decades past, it's always been the realm of the mother that seems most influential (regardless of whether it's the bride's or groom's mother). The mothers sit in the front row, often in the first seat; the mothers are honored at the wedding by being among the last to be seated before the bride walks down the aisle; and now, in our modern times, the mothers are often brought center stage as active and honored participants in the ceremony itself. Here are just a few ways you can play a large part in the ceremony, rightfully so as the mother of the groom:

* **Walking down the aisle:** Traditionally, the mother of the groom has been escorted down the aisle right before the mother of the bride, often by her husband or by one of her other children. These days, it's very common for the mother of the groom (or both parents of the groom) to walk the groom down the aisle, escorting him into a new phase of his life in much the same way that the bride's parents will escort her to the altar or chuppah.

* **Lighting the unity candle:** In the unity candle ceremony, both mothers will be called up to light two individual candlesticks, which the couple will later use to light the one unity candle to symbolize their "two lights shining as one," the joining together of their souls.

* **Performing readings:** You, as the mother of the groom, might be asked to come forward and read a selection, poem, passage of scripture, or even a writing created by the couple as a way to convey the deep meaning of their union; that you're reading it will make it even more special.

* **Conducting special tributes:** In some personalized wedding ceremonies, you might be asked to light a special candle in memory of departed family members, or to say a few words about how the departed family members are present with you all in spirit. You might be asked to lay a wreath or present a floral arrangement for the same purpose, or even to release live doves or butterflies.

* **Performing music:** To the couple, having you sing a song as part of their ceremony could be perfect if you have a nice singing voice. Some couples have asked their mothers (or fathers) to play the guitar, the piano, even tribal drums in Native-American-inspired ceremonies. Having you bring music to their ceremony could be very meaningful to the bride and groom and a special part of the event for everyone in attendance . . . and

it allows you to lend your talents to the day as part of your gift to the couple.

* **Performing ethnic or religious rituals.** If your family's religious background or heritage allows you to bring a rich depth of meaning to the wedding ceremony—such as crowning the bride and groom with olive leaves or floral wreaths the same way you were crowned at your wedding—this ritual brings an important sense of family and history to the ceremony. In some cultures, parents and grandparents are asked to present bread, wine, and salt to the couple in an Old-World offering for prosperity, health, and flavor in their future together. Assist the couple in researching any familial rituals that they might consider weaving into their rites, and know that you are very honored to be asked to be a part of them.

* **Drinking wine:** No, not from a flask right before you walk down the aisle, but as a part of some new wedding ceremonies, where the couple and their parents drink from a symbolic chalice of wine to mark that you are all "drinking from the same cup" of blessing.

Where to Research Ceremony Rituals

You can always do a simple Google search, but many people planning groups get answers by contacting the national association of their heritage or official sites from their religions. Ask the learned experts for pointers, books, articles, and advice, and they will be happy to help spread the word about their most treasured rituals and see them continue to flourish in our culture.

The Wedding Couple Pays *You* Tribute

It's ironic that today, when the bride and groom's parents might have a smaller role in planning the wedding, there seems to be an even greater emphasis by couples to pay tribute to their parents. Perhaps it's because we've returned to a greater sense of gratitude in our culture post–9/11, where adult children are very conscious of the importance of family and paying tribute to their guiding forces.

That said, don't be surprised to learn that the couple plans to pay you a special tribute during the ceremony. In today's ceremonies, it's common to find the bride and groom offering their mothers single, long-stemmed roses at some point during the ceremony. In the Catholic ceremony, for instance, the bride might offer both mothers a rose from a larger bouquet and then walk over to place the remainder of the bouquet in front of the icon of the Virgin Mother. Thus, you're honored as a mother—and in impressive company.

Here are some additional ways couples are embellishing their ceremonies with a thankful, inclusive bow to their parents:

- Marrying in the same church where the parents married
- Using the same readings the parents used
- Using the same music the parents used
- Combining elements from the bride's parents' wedding and the groom's parents' wedding
- Using an heirloom wedding ring passed down by you, or by a grandmother, or resetting the stones from an heirloom ring, pendant, or tiara. Some brides and grooms really know how to combine their families, designing rings that include reset stones contributed by both the bride's and groom's mothers (or grandmothers, aunts, godmothers, and so on). The officiant would then share this information with all the guests, so that everyone knows the couple is wearing rings passed down through the family. It's very touching.
- In one of the newest trends, parents are honored by serving as members of the bridal party. The bride might choose the mothers to serve as "brides-

maids," while the groom might ask his father to be his best man. More and more, brides are asking their mothers to be their matrons of honor, so the roles are no longer kept separate. You might find yourself in a pink bridesmaids' gown. (Don't worry . . . as you'll see in chapter 18, bridesmaids' dresses are much more stylish today!)

* Parents are given rings of their own, perhaps birthstone rings or other forms of jewelry, during a special prayer section of the ceremony designed to pay tribute to parents and acknowledge an everlasting bond with them.

* Part if not all of the wedding ceremony is conducted in the family's native tongue.

Wedding Programs

Just like a *Playbill* at a Broadway musical or play, the printed wedding program lets guests identify the "players" in the wedding party—who the musical performers are and the name of that beautiful song, the director's (read officiant's) name, and what's coming up in each unfolding "act." The program keeps guests in the know, particularly when any cultural or religious rituals are taking place. A short description of why the bride and groom are wearing crowns of olive leaves or catching figs thrown to them by the grandparents allows guests to understand and appreciate the symbolism of such rituals. Explanation makes the ceremony more meaningful for all.

Other elements to include in the wedding program:

* A description of who the bridal party members are, not just their names. As an example: John Smith, the groom's best man and former college roommate or Sarah Gale, who first introduced the bride and groom. Giving a little background on the major players informs guests and also may facilitate mingling.

* A thank-you note from the couple, thanking their parents and helpers for their work on the wedding and also thanking guests for traveling so far to share this day with them

- Poetry that's important to the couple—perhaps the first poem the groom ever wrote for the bride
- The story of the couple's engagement, such as *"Dan proposed to Elaine at sunset on the beach at Cape Cod. Onlookers applauded, and the happy couple was surprised to find they had an audience!"*
- The couple's new home address, phone number, and e-mail
- A picture of the couple
- Various decorative graphics, perhaps tying in the theme of the wedding or the destination wedding's location

Having Programs Made

While the couple can order their programs from a stationer, printer, graphic designer, or online site, it's incredibly easy (and less expensive!) to make them as a do-it-yourself project. In fact, this is one task that many grooms are happy to take on:

> *"My fiancée wrote out all the wording for the program, and I just took that file and did the layout on the computer. It was the perfect collaboration for us, and we were so happy to be able to create our programs ourselves." —Brian, groom*

Of course, this might be a job that *you* can do, too. Whoever is sitting in front of the keyboard, here are the steps to creating wonderful wedding programs for the big day:

1. Draft the wording for the entire program. Make sure to spell all the names and titles correctly—double-check with the couple—and be certain that no one has been left out. Consider adding a quote from the couple, or their favorite quote from someone else, as part of the design.

2. Buy beautiful paper—pretty, hued card stock or paper designed with graphics and borders, with great texture—at a stationer, office supply or

craft store, or online at specialty paper companies. You can find great imported papers like Egyptian linen, rice paper, vellums, overlays, and even metallic colors.

3. Choose and download graphics either from a clips site or from a digital camera.

4. Use your home computer's layout program to design each page of the program. Use decorative fonts and colored inks (experiment with a few different ones) and then print out one copy on plain paper or on the official paper to see how the spacing looks. Play with the layout to get it just right.

5. Consider enfolding each collated group of pages in a purchased wedding program cover, which you can find at office supply stores, craft stores, online, or (a great source!) religious bookstores.

6. Recruit a team of helpers to collate, fold, and assemble the programs.

7. Add a flourish, such as a ribbon to tie the packet together, theme-appropriate or colored foil stickers with the couple's monogram on the cover, or even the handwritten "autograph" of the couple on each program (a very personalized touch!). Some couples enclose a color-coordinated tissue in a folded pocket of the program—it will come in handy during the ceremony when tears start flowing!

8. Assign people to bring and distribute the programs at the wedding.

How's Your Aim?

After the ceremony the bride and groom will run through a veritable storm of birdseed, bubbles . . . throwing small objects at the couple is a way of "showering" them with blessings for their first steps as husband and wife.

This is another place where you can make a contribution to the wedding plans—the researching, buying, making, or even labeling of the various "toss-its" your guests will throw at the happy couple. So if this task falls to you, check out the market for the following possibilities:

- Birdseed in a tiny tulle pouch, tied at the top with a ribbon
- Rose petals, loosely held in paper cones or pouches
- Bottles of bubble solution with tiny screw-top wands. Look for these in craft stores for great bulk prices, and just affix a personalized label to each bottle.
- A pair of small jingle bells attached to a square of card stock, imprinted with the couple's names and instructions to "ring in" their first moments as husband and wife. Guests would then just ring the bells as the couple runs or walks by.
- Pinwheels decorated with ribbon curls and personalized stickers
- The printed words to a song that everyone can sing as the couple goes by. "That's Amore" was recently a big hit at a family wedding, with guests serenading the happy couple *before* the first bottle of champagne had been opened.

The Do-Not-Use List

Many sites have restrictions about what you can and cannot use for the wedding toss-its. Concerned about cleanup, the safety of guests, and apparently the danger to any birds or wildlife that might eat the scattered toss-its, strict rules might be in place against the following:

- Rice
- Confetti
- Flower petals
- Streamers
- Spray string
- Snowballs (Kidding on this snowball listing, but it's still not a wise idea.)

CHAPTER 8

Invitations and Printed Cards

SOMETHING WONDERFUL happens when a wedding invitation shows up in the mail. The oversize envelope with the calligraphy script . . . the Love stamp . . . the beautiful invitation that slides out of its holder to formally announce the impending wedding. The invitation brings with it a palpable sense of excitement about the event to come!

If you are consulted for this part of the wedding plans, choosing gorgeous invitations, then you have some work to do. After all, it's not just about picking a pretty invitation style out of a catalog. A lot more goes into it than that. Consider this:

The wedding invitation does far more than simply provide date, time, and place. The chosen design and wording tell the guest much more, including what the formality and style of the wedding will be. The location, such as a marina address or an estate name, tells them that this is not going to be just any wedding. Using the information they glean from the invitation, guests know how to dress for the wedding, whether or not the men will have to rent tuxes, what kind of weather to prepare for, and what kind of celebration is at hand. These particular things are very important, and the more information the invitation conveys, the better.

And, of course, there is the design: What kind of paper will the invitation be on? What colors will you use? Will you go traditional or custom-made? With graphics, or clean and elegant with just formal black script? In today's weddings, invitations offer so many lovely design choices that it can be hard to narrow down the top contenders to five, even ten!

Then there's the wording. Are people still using "honour" and "favour"? How will the parents' names be listed on the invitation as hosts? Have the rules of invitation wording changed?

The couple has quite a world of choice ahead—comprised of many different smaller decisions—when it comes to perfecting the design of these pretty papers. If you're assisting with this task, you can help make the selection a bit easier or even guide the couple as they custom-design their own invitations.

This chapter describes the steps through each choice, from design to wording, to help the bride and groom get to the point where holding their finalized invitation in their hands brings *them* a palpable sense of excitement about the event to come as well! For many couples, the arrival of their wedding invitations is one of the first times they realize the wedding is really going to happen. The invitation is the first tangible thing for the wedding day that has been created. That's when they get excited.

So now it's time for *you* to get excited about the task at hand—helping to design and choose invitations and the many other printed items that will be used for the wedding.

Traditional or Nontraditional

While it's true that brides and grooms of today are shrugging off many traditional rules for weddings—second-time brides wear white gowns without a second thought, many marriages take place in a nonreligious location, both parents walk the bride and the groom down the aisle—invitations are one area where etiquette still stands strong. Many couples want to adhere to those age-old rules about correct wording and design for formal wedding invitations. They are looking up models of traditional wording, and they are asking their parents and their wedding coordinators for help. *Or* they're using some elements of traditional wedding invitations, but incorporating them into more modern, creative invitation designs. Wedding invitation experts tell me the rules are bending, but they will never break. Design is flexible; wording—at least for formal weddings—is traditional. Here is where you can also chime in with the answers your son and his bride need.

Selection of Invitation Elements

The creation of one wedding invitation comes after a few dozen decisions have been made about the kind of paper you'll use, the wording, the layout, and so on. Here we'll take each issue one at a time, leading you to the finished product.

Paper Stock

For most wedding invitations, formal or informal, you'll find a thicker card stock to be standard. For formal or ultraformal weddings, the choice is usually an ecru-colored card stock as the foundation of the wedding invitation, with formal black lettering in formal script. That's the traditional model.

In this wonderful world of creative invitations, and in our global world of artistry, you'll discover fabulous imported papers from around the world—textured papers, glossy papers, rice papers from Japan, and papers from Ecuador, the Philippines, India, Thailand, Australia, South Africa, Egypt, and China. Check online to discover great sources of artisan-class papers and card stock, or check at office supply stores for a wide range of formal card stocks and invitation papers.

Printing Styles

Formal invitations professionally ordered are most often printed using standard thermography, which gives it that formal appearance in smooth, crisp print. A more formal, and more expensive, option is engraving, a professional process in which the letters are raised. Most couples choose thermography over engraving, as the effect is quite similar in formality. If invitations will be made on your home computer, a crisp black print gives much the same effect as thermography, only in nonshiny type.

Color

Today's couples are using color in their invitations, even for formal weddings. From colored card stock rather than traditional ecru, to colored print for the wording, it's a way for them to be more individual, more creative, and even give a nod to the theme and season of their wedding; for example, many couples who are planning beach weddings choose a sandy beige invitation card with teal or sea blue lettering. For a winter wedding, invitation experts are creating more styles on ice blue paper with platinum ink to give a "wintry" feel. Christmastime and Valentine's Day weddings call out for invitations printed on bright red paper with silver ink. Springtime weddings might beckon for lavender print on cream-colored paper or deeper rose print on a blush-pink stock. Color provides more visual impact for invitations, and that's the biggest trend right now. So look for color in both paper stock *and* in lettering.

Fonts

Speaking of lettering, the letter style in which the words will be printed is the *font*, and there are hundreds of fonts to choose from. Consider the following examples:

Arial
Baskerville Old Face
Book Antiqua
Brush Script

The options are vast, so be sure to look closely at the font samples on any order form, Web site, or on your home computer. The most important factor is to be sure the font you choose will make all of the information clear and legible, so that guests can get the *correct* information from the invitation. If the print isn't clear, guests may read the wedding date and location wrong; for instance, in some more decorative fonts with swirls and flourishes, 0s can look like 9s, 1s can look like 7s, and Ts can look like Ps. Be sure that every word on the invitation will be clear to the reader—that the fonts are not only pretty, but that they work.

You can design the invitations to have two different kinds of fonts, one for the wording of the invitation and another to make the bride and groom's names stand out. Some couples ask for the decorative swirly print to announce the wedding, and then a more functional block print to convey the wedding location, time, and date. In most cases, it will not cost extra to use two different fonts on one invitation, so ask any printer about the standard no-charge-for-two offers you've heard about.

And, finally, always see a proof of your designed invitation before you place the order. Online invitation-ordering sites can show you exactly what your designed invitation will look like, but seeing it on a screen is not the same as seeing the real thing. Most invitation companies will put in an order for a proof of *one* copy of your invitation, printed on plain paper, so you can get a good look at what you're about to order. Some companies, Birchcraft for example, will send you a proof on your chosen card stock, at a charge of about $20, and many couples tell me it's worth spending the extra money to see the real thing. Some couples order proofs of several different designs of invitations, and then choose their favorite.

It's All About the Wording

We've discussed design for the wedding invitation, and now it's time to get into the most important part: the wording.

As I'm sure you're aware, there is a ton of Old-World etiquette involved in the wording of formal wedding invitations, some of it with origins in Elizabethan England. We may like to be progressive, but we nevertheless value tradition. That's why, as I mentioned at the opening of this chapter, couples want to get the formal wording correct.

It's a matter of being proper, but it's also a matter of paying due respect to the hosts of the wedding (that could be you). Couples break out in a sweat when it's time to arrange the wording of their invitations: If both sets of parents helped equally with the wedding, is it fair to go by tradition and list the bride's family first? What if the groom's family did more to plan the wedding? Do they break with tradition and list the groom's family first? How many people will that offend? What if the bride and groom are paying for the wedding? Won't their parents get mad if they're left off the invitation and the couple is listed on the host line? Won't that be embarrassing? What if one set of parents is divorced or both sets are divorced? What if some parents are remarried and others aren't? Do they list the stepparents? *Aaaaargh!* The headaches that are created by this one line on the invitation—or the prospect of four lines to list all the parents—can be enough to drive a young couple to drink.

Little Extras for Pretty Design

Here are a few of the more creative accents to wedding invitations today:

- Monograms: Very hot for weddings right now is to use the couple's initials entwined in a formal monogram that will be used as a wedding-décor theme.

- Ribbon ties: These are placed at the top of invitation cards or are used to seal the sides of a double-panel card.

- Pretty borders: A pearlized border outside the invitation edges, framing the wording or accenting the areas of the invitation; a swirl of black graphic print like a Victorian picture frame; floral designs like a string of tiny pink roses; colored borders.

- Overlays: A formal or graphic invitation looks lovely when covered with a sheer vellum in a shaded color or with a graphic design, such as ice blue snowflakes on the vellum laid over a pristine white invitation card. The added effect conveys the winter wedding, and the invitation itself remains formal. The overlay provides a dash of color and style to make invitations more visually impressive.

- Graphics: Many professionally ordered wedding invitations now come with beautiful graphics, like sunsets, sandcastles, roses or calla lilies, or even a photo of the couple.

Of course, you might not *care* if you're listed second on the invitation, owing to your respect for tradition, and thus you can completely relieve the couple's fears. You'll get a big gold star for that. The "cooler" you are about your place on the invitation, the better the entire event will go. You know you contributed to the wedding. You know you helped plan it. You don't need to be *first*, like a spoiled five-year-old. But that's you. Sometimes the bride and groom are dealing with *other* family members who will throw a tantrum when the invitations don't conform to their expectations.

To bring a little clarity, here are the "official" models of how today's couples should arrange the wording of the invitations.

The traditional model, when the bride's parents host:

> *Mr. and Mrs. Steven Smith*
> *request the honour of your company*
> *at the marriage of their daughter*
> *Sarah Anne*
> *to*
> *Mr. Michael Thomas Jones,*
> *son of Mr. and Mrs. Thomas Jones*
> *Saturday, the sixth of June*
> *at four o'clock in the afternoon*
> *Saint Mary's Church*
> *Baltimore, Maryland*

If the bride's parents are divorced:

Mr. John Smith

and

Mrs. Leslie Parker Smith

(or Mrs. Leslie Parker if she has reverted to her maiden name)

request the honour of your presence

at the marriage of their daughter

Lisa Marie

and

Mr. Jeffrey Lawrence Black

son of

Mr. and Mrs. Lawrence Black

Saturday, the twenty-fifth of May

If both sets of parents are hosting:

Mr. and Mrs. Arnold Kelly

and

Mr. and Mrs. Kevin Michaels

request the honour of your presence

at the marriage of their children

Paige Amanda

and

Aaron Scott

Saturday, the fifteenth of May

If multiple sets of parents are hosting (such as with adoptive parents, birth parents, stepparents, and so on):

The loving parents of

Tania Gayle Sanders

and

Justin Alexander Brady

request the honour of your company . . .

If the bride and groom are hosting the wedding:

Ms. Emily Rae Stevens

and

Mr. Miles Evan Stoianovic

Request the honour of your presence

As they unite in marriage

Saturday, the twenty-fifth of May

For more samples of invitation wording, visit www.weddingchannel.com.

Spelling and Titles Count

Here are some guidelines on the little wording issues that can trip you up:

When Do You Use Honour *and* Favour?

That's one of the tricky little etiquette loops that confuses people planning formal wedding invitations. They've seen ones with *honour* spelled with the *our* and without it. What's the difference? Where does "request the pleasure of your company" fit in? Here's the official ruling on that one: When a wedding will be held inside a house of worship such as a church or synagogue, the proper wording is "... request the honour of your presence" (or *honor* if you choose not to use the

Old-World spelling). When the wedding will be held outside of an official house of worship, use "request the pleasure of your company."

It's Doctor *Thomas!*

Whenever you're addressing anyone in print, whether on the invitation or on the envelope, be sure you have the correct spelling of each guest's name, as well as his or her title, if any. And use full titles: Dr. Thomas would be *Doctor Thomas.* Capt. Jones would be *Captain Jones.* Together with his wife, it would be *Captain and Mrs. John Jones.*

Don't Abbreviate Anything

All formal invitations require the usual abbreviations to be spelled out. Use *Street,* not St., *Avenue,* not Ave., and so on. States are spelled out as are cities like *New York City.*

Time

No, you can't say 4 P.M. for the time of the wedding. It's *four o'clock in the afternoon, seven o'clock in the evening,* or *eleven o'clock in the morning.*

International Invitations

Couples with family in far-flung countries, or those with relatives who do not speak English, are having a portion of their wedding invitations created in the family language, translated by an expert and artistically produced. Those distant cousins will be grateful!

Invitations on CD-ROM?

Technology is a big part of wedding plans: many couples do most of their research and ordering online, set up wedding Web sites, and communicate with guests about bridal registries, hotels, and airlines via e-mail. It's only natural that technology should come knocking on the invitation's door, too. While some couples are going hi-tech with their invitations, recording them with expertly edited graphics, titles, and soundtracks as mini-movies to convey all the necessary information to their guests, this format is not yet totally acceptable. After all, there may be relatives who might not have access to a CD-ROM player, or they might not be up on technology in the first place. But for couples whose guests are guaranteed to be computer-savvy, this option could be a winner. Look into professional CD-ROM creation, or use the services of someone on your team who knows how to make them. Or check out the wedding-invitation software package from www.mountaincow.com, with its thirty sample templates, twelve fonts, countless graphics, *and* the ability to download your own address book for easy invitation addressing.

E-mail Invitations

Sites like evite.com do have wedding invitations online, which you can e-mail to the guest list, with RSVP messages coming to the site with the number of Yes, No, and Maybe responses tabulated. Again, some couples are fine with the informal and efficient mode of e-mail invitations—it's a personal choice most often acceptable for informal and casual weddings—but many prefer the official look of printed invitations. Talk to your team and see if this free option works for you.

Informal Invitations

For very informal wedding invitations, including those for some beach weddings and destination affairs, the couple might choose to throw formality to the tropical breeze and create unique wording. I've seen couples word their invitations in poetry, or in fun and funky celebratory style. ("We're sailing off into the sunset, and we'd like you to join us. So meet us at Pier 4 at Seabreeze Marina and we'll have the champagne waiting for you!") This informal new voice in wedding invitations gives the guests a taste of the style of the party to come (informal celebration on a yacht, so don't wear stilettos) and it brings the couple's voices and fun-loving personalities to the fore.

Invitation Inserts

Within your invitations mailing, you'll need to include any number of additional printed cards and information. Look at designs for the following, and order them in a matching card stock to create a fully coordinated invitation packet:

- **Reception card:** This is a separate invitation to the reception, including the location and time.

- **Response card:** Guests use this to respond with their acceptance or regrets, and, perhaps, their checked-off choice of the entrée they wish to be served at the reception.

- **Response envelope:** Guests use this stamped, self-addressed card to return their response card to the hosts.

- **Printed notice of hotel reservations and contact information:** This might include a link to the hotel's reservations site, with the code number for your party's reserved block of rooms. Smart hosts provide hotel information for two or three area hotels so that guests can choose the distance and room rate they want.

- **Printed notice of your wedding Web site** (if applicable): A separate printed card can invite guests to visit the couple's wedding Web site. (Some couples print this information on their Save-the-Date card.)

- **Printed directions or a detailed map to your ceremony and reception sites:** You can either get these preprinted from the wedding site or the hotel (most of these can provide you with stacks of printed directions as a service), or you can create them using a site like MapQuest. Or have a talented artist friend with a good sense of direction create maps with great graphics for use in the invitation packet. This original map can be the artist's wedding gift to the couple.

- **At-Home card:** This small card provides the couple's new address, phone number, and e-mail for after the wedding, and also officially informs guests about the bride's choice of name change: whether she's taking the groom's surname, retaining her surname or hyphenating the two.

Other Printed Items

So much will be going into print! For the entirety of the wedding weekend, you'll need a large number of cards, signs, and other printed items to serve and inform your guests, spread the joy, and say thank you. Here is a guideline of the types of printed items you can either order or easily make on your own using your handy home computer and some great card stock from an office supply store:

- **Wedding-weekend itineraries:** These give guests the full schedule, locations, time, and dress codes of the various planned events during the wedding weekend.

- **Invitations to the rehearsal:** All the major players need to know where and when it will be.

- **Invitations to the rehearsal dinner:** These may go to the bridal party and major players of the wedding, plus a selection of out-of-town guests you wish to include in that night's festivities.

- **Seating place cards:** These are for the rehearsal dinner and the reception.

- **Table number or name cards:** These cards can feature graphics, or just giant script numbers/names.

- **Menu cards:** These are placed on each guest table, listing the names and descriptions of the courses to come during the meal. This gets guests excited about the menu.

- **Dish identification cards:** If the site doesn't do it as a service to your guests, perhaps you'll choose to print up cards letting guests know what each item on the buffet table is, or which possibilities the chef can create at each pasta, seafood, or carving station.

- **Bar cards:** Printed and perhaps laminated and displayed on the bar, these let guests know the selection of mixed drinks, wines, beers, or soft drinks you've selected as part of the beverage service. Some couples give their mixed drinks personalized names, which would be printed on this card.

- **Welcome messages for guest hotel-room gift baskets:** These will accompany a hospitality basket you'll have delivered to any out-of-town guests' rooms. As they unwrap the goodies you've given them, they'll also get a lovely welcome note from the couple.

- **Directional signs:** These can be posted to let guests know the cocktail party is "this way," or the coat check is "that way." Always a good thing to have at alternative wedding locations or outdoor sites that must be accessed through a short walk down a pathway or down stairs.

- **Favor cards:** A printed message from the bride and groom can accompany any favors they'll have guests take home after the wedding. These can be done on stickers or on cards.

- **Wedding announcements:** These can be sent out to additional friends and family after the wedding (or the elopement).

- **Thank-you notes:** These will be needed after the wedding.

- **And don't forget magnets!** Now, couples are sending some of their printed items in magnet form, like Save-the-Date Cards and even thank-yous with a picture of them; these function as keepsake items as well (see www.psaessentials.com for more on this creative print idea).

Expert Tips to Make Your Wedding Invitations Special

Leslie Vismara, chief designer and founder of Vismara Invitations, shares ideas:

With relatives and friends scattered all over, every wedding is a destination event, whether in a backyard, vineyard, meadow, or on a mountainside or beach. Put yourself in your guests' places when planning and announcing your event with save-the-date cards, invitations, and travel information.

Keep these thoughts—and feelings—in mind when you plan the special day:

* While invitations may seem like a small part of the wedding, they shouldn't be an afterthought. Invitations and announcement cards are the very first impression of the wedding and set the tone for the day—whether relaxed, formal, elegant, or outdoors.

* Because many of the guests won't be in the same town where the wedding is to be held, put yourself in their shoes:
  — *Save-the-Date cards*: Be sure to send a save-the-date card as far in advance as possible so they can schedule vacation and travel arrangements.
  — *Create an invitation package*: Some couples include a photo of themselves in the invitation and make the invitation into a little booklet with maps and information about what is planned for the weekend.

- — ***What to do at the wedding destination***: Gather information about the location of the wedding and activities there.
- — ***Create a map to include with the invitation***: Show guests how to find all of the wedding events, and provide information about how much time it will take to get there. Let them know if they will need to rent a car or will be able to carpool with other guests.
- — ***Consider inviting out-of-town guests to the rehearsal dinner***: Traveling guests have come a long way to celebrate with you.

* Save-the-Date cards are a casual announcement of the upcoming celebration. Make them fun by relating them to the theme of the wedding, such as by using themes related to the location of the event: Hints like flowers, leaves, or architectural details are good.

* Have fun with the design/appearance: It's an important event, and it's a celebration—have fun with it! Save-the-Date cards and invitations should reflect the couple's identity. Use words, colors, and papers to add personality when setting the tone for your special day. After spending so much time finding the perfect site, use it as the inspiration for the invitation. Look around at the flowers, trees, scenery, and other details to help select a theme that can be carried through from the invitation to the ceremony itself:
  - — Start with the couple's favorite color for the ink on the invitation.
  - — Speckled paper with sea blue ink for beach weddings.

— Green ink and ivory colored paper for weddings in forests, on mountains, or at lodge resorts.

— White paper with metallic silver ink for a winter wedding in the mountains.

— Let guests know what kind of event it is. If the ceremony is outside in the mountains, tell them to "leave stiletto heels at home and bring a favorite sweater."

— Use favorite quotes: These can relate to the couple's personality or something fun about marriage.

— Add space to the RSVP card for guests to comment: There's a good chance lots of enthusiastic messages will be received.

— Add humor to the RSVP card: Phrases like "Sorry to say we'll miss the day" are lighthearted.

Vismara Invitations is based in Denver, Colorado, and specializes in themed invitations and wedding stationery. View the full line by visiting www. vismarainvitations.com. Printed with permission from Leslie Vismara of Vismara Invitations.

To get you started on your search for great invitations, invitation ideas, colors, and ways to personalize them, as well as ideas for your additional printed items, here are a few of my all-time favorite invitation Web sites:

Botanical Paperworks: www.botanicalpaperworks.com
Invitations 4 Sale: www.invitations4sale.com
Love Luck and Angels: www.loveluckandangels.com
PSA Essentials: www.psaessentials.com
Vismara Invitations: www.vismarainvitations.com

CHAPTER 9

Bouquets, Corsages, and Boutonnieres

RIGHT NOW, THE BRIDE is dreaming of her bouquet . . .

It might be a tight cluster of calla lilies . . . or a collection of white roses interspersed with gardenias or peace lilies . . . or a bunch of wildflowers . . . or a burst of color in bright red or purple.

Of course, the bride decides on her bouquet and her flowers, but she will likely include you and her mom in the enjoyable girls' day out to visit florists, nurseries, or even flower shows to scout out the perfect blooms for her big day. One bride wrote to tell me about how she took both mothers with her to the annual Philadelphia Flower Show. It was a research outing and a way to bond over the beautiful floral scenery in the convention hall.

Since the flower search is one of the areas most brides share with the moms, your chances of being in on this lovely task are good. Here is some guidance on the selection of all things floral for the wedding day.

Your Shopping List

First, know exactly what you're shopping for: how many bouquets, how many boutonnieres, and the décor the bride and groom have in mind for the sites and events. The following is a shopping checklist, with space at the bottom to fill in any additional pieces required:

_____ Bride's bouquet

_____ Bridesmaids' bouquets

_____ Flowers for the flowergirl (either a basket, a nosegay, loose petals, or a floral wreath for her hair)

_____ Corsages for the mothers

_____ Corsages for the grandmothers

_____ Corsages for other special women (godmothers, guardians, and so on)

_____ Boutonnieres for the groom, ushers, fathers, grandfathers, and other special men

_____ Floral décor for the ceremony site

    _____ Altar décor

    _____ Pew décor

    _____ Flowers to be placed on individual seats

    _____ Tribute bouquets and stems

    _____ Pedestal floral arrangements

_____ Floral décor for the reception site

    _____ Centerpieces for guest tables

    _____ Centerpieces for the head table or sweethearts' table

    _____ Floral arrangements for the buffet tables and stations

    _____ Floral arrangements for the cake table

    _____ Floral arrangements for the gift table

    _____ Floral arrangements for any tables where photographs are displayed

    _____ Floral arrangements for restrooms

_____ Flowers for the rehearsal dinner

    _____ Flowers for the bride

    _____ Flowers for the bride's mother (and for you!)

_____ Corsages

_____ Boutonnieres

_____ Centerpieces and décor

_____ Thank-you bouquets or flowers for any participants in the wedding day

_____ Floral arrangements to brighten out-of-town guests' rooms

_____ Flowers to decorate the wedding cake

_____ Flowers to decorate the getaway car, limo, or carriage

_____ Memorial wreaths

_____ Flower petals to scatter for décor on tabletops, buffet tables, cake tables, and so on

Other items:

❧ _____

❧ _____

❧ _____

❧ _____

Items to Rent from the Florist

__ Chuppah

__ Aisle runner

__ Ring pillow

__ Trellis

__ Potted plants and potted trees

__ Pedestal stands

Looking at Individual Flowers

Once you have your shopping list in hand, you know better what you're shopping for. So now it's time to start looking at the individual flowers that will make gorgeous bouquets, centerpieces, décor elements, and boutonnieres. Many brides say that choosing their wedding flowers was not easy. There is a wealth of different types of flowers available—thousands of different varieties—and it takes some coordinating to find the loveliest ones that will be obtainable at the time of the wedding, in good supply, and reasonably priced.

Here are the main wedding-flower shopping rules:

1. Find out which flowers will be in season at the time of the wedding. I love the flower-selection interactive tool at www.blissweddings.com, the wedding floral generator, which allows you to plug in the season of your wedding and then tells you which kinds of flowers are in season at that time of the year. Also, www.romanticflowers.com has a similar chart, and you can find out more about seasonal supplies for your region by talking to a local florist.

2. Find out which flowers are grown locally versus flowers that have to be imported from New Zealand, Hawaii, South Africa, or other countries. You can get any kind of flower you want for the wedding, but if it has to be imported, it's going to cost you more. Ask about local versus imported flowers, and check the Web sites listed above for more on regional availability.

3. Look at nontraditional wedding flowers as opposed to traditional wedding flowers like roses, gardenias, calla lilies, and orchids. Especially in peak season, looking "outside the box" at less "bridal" wedding blooms could net you unique flowers for less. Some of my favorites in the alternative flower market are anemones and a unique flower called Astrantia, which looks like a starburst and comes in rose silver or greenish silver. Just gorgeous.

4. Use lots of greenery. Extra greenery gives a natural, woodsy feel to the room, like something out of Shakespeare's *A Midsummer Night's Dream*.

Greenery is relatively inexpensive compared to flowers, and it gives a lush feel to décor.

5. Supplement fewer showstopping flowers with unique items, like fruits, flowering branches, gourds, pinecones, shells, even stones. These natural items are increasingly popular in the wedding décor field. At one summertime wedding, the bride and groom used bowls overflowing with whole lemons and limes as their centerpieces—each one cost about $7— and it was a great coordination with the wedding's color scheme and tropical theme.

6. Accent the flowers with pretty touches. Your florist can insert pearl-head pushpins into the centers of roses and flowers for a little bit of extra shine. Some brides opt for crystal pushpins to lend their flowers some extra light-catching elements.

7. Borrow design ideas from magazines, Web sites, florists' design books, and catalogs. One bride from California tells me that she got the inspiration for her centerpieces from a Pottery Barn catalog. Others borrow the styles they see in magazines' celebrity-wedding issues. No matter where the images come from, your floral designer should be able to create bouquets and centerpieces that are exactly what the bride and groom want.

8. Also, many brides want their wedding day flowers to be extra-special. That could mean using the same kinds of flowers their mothers and future mothers-in-law had in *their* bouquets on their wedding days, using the favorite flowers of their mothers and grandmothers, or using the kind of flower their groom bought them early in their relationship. These brides want their flowers to have meaning, not just beauty.

Your Corsage

In years past, the mothers of the bride and groom would wear pretty floral corsages pinned to their dress or jacket tops as a way to say, I am the mom. Now, moms are still given special floral pieces to wear for the wedding day, but they're a little bit different. I spoke with Casey Cooper, the principal designer and owner of Botanicals in Chicago (www.botanicalschicago.com), who says that the new designs for moms are floral bracelets and floral chokers, delicate ribbon-tied pieces with small flowers or a grander flower, which has more of a jewelry look than we've seen in the past. Moms tell me this choice is more stylish, less cumbersome, and leaves no holes in their dresses. One mom even told me, "Now it doesn't look like I'm going to a prom."

Boutonnieres for the Men

The look in men's boutonnieres is unique and elegant, and smaller. Baby rosebuds are popular, as are sprigs of stephanotis—with the groom wearing a slightly larger bunching of flowers than those worn by his men. The fathers and grandfathers may also sport these lapel-enhancers, and today's creative couples are choosing different types of lapel flowers for each man in the bridal party. This provides the men with a unique element in their otherwise uniform attire.

A Site to Visit . . .

As mentioned earlier, Blissweddings.com has an interactive tool that provides the names of flowers that will be in season at the time of the wedding. This tool also gives you a list of flowers broken down by the following:

- The color of flower (as in, "all white" or "multi")
- Flowers native to particular regions
- A cross-reference of in-season and regionally grown flowers
- Suggestions for flowers and colors to coordinate with the bridesmaids' dresses, and thus also your dress

It's excellent! So make use of this site's tool, and help the bride find perfect ideas for her wedding day blooms.

CHAPTER 10

Capturing the Moment

NO DOUBT EVERYONE will want to remember the wedding day forever, and that's why couples spend so much money on their photographers and videographers. As the mother of the groom, you know that every moment is precious, and no amount of money is too much to spend on such an important future investment. After all, the couple's future children, your grandchildren, are going to be looking at these images! So they had better be taken by talented professionals, and those professionals had better get every important shot!

Before we get into the nitty-gritty of choosing and hiring wedding photographers and videographers—which, by the way, the groom and the fathers may be eager to help out with—here is a helpful checklist that you can use to request and get the type of footage—both still and video—that you want. You can tear out these pages and give them as a wish list to the photo experts you hire:

The Bride's and Groom's Preparation for the Big Day

_____ Bride's gown hanging in her bedroom, before the bride puts it on, with her shoes and accessories nearby

_____ Bridesmaids' arrival

_____ Bridal breakfast

Must-Have Shots Before the Wedding Day

It's not only the happenings on the actual wedding day that should be captured for posterity but also the many special moments leading up to it. Don't miss a moment!

- The engagement celebration with your family
- The engagement party
- The planning meeting with the bride's family and the couple
- Shopping for the wedding gown
- Shopping for the cake, the flowers, and other colorful events
- Bridal shower events
- Wedding weekend events where family and friends are present and having a great time in your backyard or at the park
- The rehearsal
- The rehearsal dinner
- Moments from the night before the wedding

_____ Bride and her entourage going to, or enjoying the services at, the beauty salon

_____ Bride and her entourage having a champagne toast at the beauty salon

_____ Bride and bridesmaids getting ready for the wedding

_____ Mom or maid of honor helping bride attach her veil or button the last button on her gown

_____ Dad's first look at the bride in her wedding attire

_____ Full-length shot of bride in her gown, from several angles, in several settings

_____ Bride and her maids, fully dressed, having a champagne toast

_____ Bride and her parents having a champagne toast

_____ Bride being given her something old, something new, something borrowed, something blue

_____ Bride's first look at her wedding bouquet as she unwraps the box

_____ Bride holding her bouquet

_____ Bride with her sibling(s)

_____ Bride with her grandparents

_____ Bride with her mother

_____ Bride with her mother and grandmother(s)

_____ Bride with her father

_____ Bride with her godmother

_____ Bride with her parents and stepparents

_____ Bride with her maid or matron of honor

_____ Bride with her bridesmaids, formal pose

_____ Bride with her bridesmaids, casual pose

_____ Bride with flower girls

_____ Bride with each of her bridesmaids, individually

_____ Bride receiving gift from the groom on the wedding morning

_____ Bride talking with groom on the phone before the wedding, to exchange last-second "I love you"s

_____ Bride and bridesmaids departing for the ceremony, posing in front of the limo or waving from the window as the car pulls away from the curb

_____ Mothers, fathers, and relatives departing for the ceremony

_____ Groom in casual attire, hanging out with his buddies before the wedding, perhaps getting breakfast or playing golf

_____ Groom getting ready for the wedding, assisted by his best man or his father as they work on his tie

_____ Groomsmen getting ready

_____ Best man hugging the groom

_____ Groom with his parents and/or stepparents

_____ Groom with his siblings

_____ Groom with his groomsmen

_____ Groom and groomsmen putting on their boutonnieres

_____ Groom getting a high-five from the ring bearer

_____ Groom and his men departing for the ceremony

_____ Groom hugging his dad before the ceremony

_____ Groom giving the thumbs-up sign as he arrives at the ceremony site

_____ Bride and her parents en route to the ceremony (in the limousine, looking out the window as the car or carriage makes its way to the site)

_____ Bride arriving at the ceremony site

_____ Father helping the bride out of the car

_____ Any facial expressions that pass between parents and daughter at that time (hopefully, excitement!)

At the Ceremony

_____ A picture of the empty ceremony site before guests arrive

_____ A wide-angle shot of the ceremony site from a balcony as the guests arrive

_____ Guests arriving and being seated

_____ Special guests being escorted to their seats

_____ Ushers escorting mothers to their seats (Christian wedding)

_____ Footage of the bride waiting in the foyer, listening to the music, until it's her time to walk down the aisle

_____ Footage of the groom and his buddies waiting nervously for it to be time

_____ Footage of the bride with her parents, preparing to walk down the aisle

_____ Groom and groomsmen taking their place at the altar

_____ Bridesmaids walking down the aisle

_____ Flower girl and/or ring bearer walking down the aisle

_____ Maid of honor walking down the aisle

_____ Grandparents walking down the aisle (in a Jewish wedding)

_____ Bride and her parents walking down the aisle

_____ A close-up of the groom's face when he first sees his bride (not to be missed!)

_____ A close-up of the bride's face when she first sees her groom (also a priceless moment!)

_____ Bride and parents meeting with the groom at the altar

_____ Groom and bride's father shaking hands before the presentation of the bride to the groom

_____ Bride and groom taking hands at the altar

_____ Wide-angle shot from the balcony capturing the moment the bride and groom take their places at the altar, including the guests in their seats

_____ Bride and groom listening to the officiant speak

_____ Readings and musical performances

_____ Mothers lighting the unity candle

_____ Bride and groom lighting the unity candle

_____ Bride and groom greeting their parents and offering peace as part of the ceremony

_____ Any religious or cultural rituals performed for the ceremony

_____ Bride and groom exchanging vows

_____ Bride and groom exchanging rings

_____ Close-up of bride's and groom's hands as they place the rings on each other's fingers

_____ Bride and groom's kiss

_____ Bride and groom turn to their applauding audience

_____ Bride and groom walk back down the aisle as husband and wife

_____ Bride and groom exit ceremony site and kiss

_____ Recessional to capture bridal party, parents, and guests greeting the couple at the exit of the ceremony site

_____ The receiving line

_____ The shower of birdseed or bubbles as the couple runs to the limousine

_____ Bride and groom leaving ceremony site with a JUST MARRIED sign on the back of the car

_____ Bride and groom standing up out of the limousine sunroof waving good-bye

_____ Bride and groom in backseat of the limousine

_____ Bridal party climbing into their limousines or onto the party bus

_____ Bride's and groom's parents hugging one another or wiping away tears as the couple departs

After the Ceremony, Before the Reception
(Note: Some couples break with tradition and take the bride-and-groom photos before the ceremony, so see what works best for the couple)

_____ Bride and groom embracing

_____ Bride and groom sealed in a kiss

_____ Bride and groom with the bride's parents

_____ Bride and groom with the groom's parents

_____ Bride and groom with both sets of parents

_____ Bride and groom with both sets of parents and both sets of grandparents

_____ Bride and groom with her grandparents

_____ Bride and groom with his grandparents

_____ Bride and groom individually with each of their grandparents

_____ Bride and groom with bride's extended family

_____ Bride and groom with groom's extended family

_____ Bride and groom with all family members

_____ Bride and groom with all of their friends

_____ Bride, groom, and all of their siblings

_____ Bride and groom with bridesmaids

_____ Bride and groom with maid of honor

_____ Bride and groom with all female attendants

_____ Bride and groom with best man

_____ Bride and groom with all groomsmen

_____ Bride and groom with entire bridal party

At the Reception

_____ Photos of the reception site outside

_____ Photos of scenery around the reception site, like the sunset

_____ Table setting

_____ Décor

_____ Sweethearts' table decorated for the happy couple

_____ Random shots of guests at the cocktail hour and beginning of reception

_____ Parents and bridal party being introduced into the room

_____ Bride and groom arriving at the reception site

_____ Bride and groom making their way to the ballroom

_____ Bride and groom making their grand entrance into the ballroom

_____ Bride and groom during their first dance

_____ Bride dancing with her father

_____ Groom dancing with his mother

_____ First full dance of the evening; photographer should capture the couples dancing

_____ Bride and groom dancing with the flower girls or ring bearer

_____ Best man's toast

_____ Maid of honor's toast

_____ Parents' toast

_____ Couple's toast

_____ Bride and groom toasting one another

_____ Close-up of the bride and groom's toasting flutes clinking together

_____ Parents dancing

_____ Bride dancing with bridesmaids

_____ Bride dancing with grandparents

_____ Kids dancing or playing—and, yes, even having a tantrum

_____ Entertainers performing

_____ Guests partying

_____ Cake

_____ Bride and groom cutting cake

_____ Bride and groom feeding each other a piece of cake

_____ Dessert table

_____ Bouquet toss

_____ Woman catching the bouquet

_____ Other women congratulating her

_____ Removal and tossing of the garter

_____ Candid shots from the evening

_____ Requested group shots

_____ Bride and groom leaving the reception, saying good-bye to special guests

_____ Scenes from the after-party

Additional Photo or Video Wish List:

❧ _____

❧ _____

❧ _____

❧ _____

❧ _____

❧ _____

❧ _____

❧ _____

Finding and Hiring Photographers and Videographers

The first step entails calling all of the people you know who have hired photographers and videographers in the recent past and asking for referrals. Get the names of professionals who delivered great pictures expeditiously, and at decent rates. Check out whether they are members of a professional association (to be sure they're accredited, trained, and have access to information on the newest technology). Then, with the bride and groom, go meet with them and look at sample albums and videos, check their price packages, inquire about their equipment and editing process, request special shots and effects, and look over their contracts.

Even more important, get a feel for the photo experts' style and personality. Each pro will have an individual approach to the craft. Some are portrait photojournalists or videojournalists and others offer more documentary style. See how you all feel with this person. Is the pro friendly and casual, or stiff and "trying too hard"? It's very important that the bride and groom feel like this is someone they're going to want in the room during the wedding. Photo and video professionals are going to be interacting with all of the guests, running the show during the significant portion of time while the portraits are being taken. So is this person's manner something everyone will want to deal with on the wedding day? Many couples have walked away from well-priced pros just because they felt rushed or spoken down to. A pro's personal style is every bit as important as his or her technical style, so be sure this is someone with whom you have no trouble establishing good rapport. Very important for the flow of the wedding day.

Going Digital?

When couples are encouraged to ask their photo professionals about the types of cameras they'll be using, and the editing system on which their pictures and videos will be produced, the first question most couples have is about digital cameras. Until recently, even photographers and videographers were wary about their own hi-tech gadgets, not knowing how digital images would last over time. Wedding professionals often advised against using digital equipment at this point until the proof could be seen.

Well, the proof is in. Today's top-of-the-line professional digital cameras have passed the test, producing perfection in the image department and allowing professionals to deliver final products quickly. Not too long ago, recently married couples had to wait months for their photos, but now photographers can post their wedding pictures within days just by uploading them onto a Web-site system (like www.PICtage.com), where the couple and all of their guests can view and order the pictures they want. You won't have to handle picture-ordering! You just send the guests to the site so they can order their own!

So whether the photographer uses a high-end 35-mm or digital camera, the results should be perfect. You're looking for great resolution and pixel size, and varied shutter speeds and special-effect lenses that can be used to create beautiful shots. With a digital camera, the photographer can see the photo right there on his camera's LCD screen, so he can tell if you blinked or if a shadow ruined the shot. This technology means that your pro can make sure he gets all the needed pictures—no surprises to come—and you're sure to be happy with the finished product.

Get Your Negatives

This is one area in which you should negotiate with your photo professionals. Get the negatives and the raw video footage signed over to you so that *you* own them. Picture pros make a lot of money when they keep the rights to the wedding pictures, and then the newlyweds have to pay a fortune to get copies made from their own wedding negatives or master tape. Be sure you get not just the negatives but also the rights. Very important.

Making Your Pictures Last

An important question with digital photos and DVDs is, How long do they last? But that's been a bigger issue with film photographs that aren't stored correctly. To keep your photos and videos from fading, yellowing, or being permanently deleted, always use the following safety steps to preserve these precious images:

- For your VHS-taped wedding video, snap off the little tab on the tape that will then make it impossible for you or anyone else to record something else—like the Super Bowl—over the wedding video.

- Don't worry about color versus black-and-whites. It used to be that color prints faded more quickly than black-and-white prints because of the chemicals used in color processing. But refinements in technology have eliminated that problem, and color photos now last just as long as black-and-white or sepia-toned pictures.

- Ask if the photo lab will rinse the prints in such a way as to be sure no chemical residue remains on the pictures. A quality lab will do an extra-thorough job with this, and the "clean" pictures will last longer.

- Hands off! When the pictures do come, even the proofs, make sure that anyone who handles them is careful not to get fingerprints on them. Oils and dirt from fingerprints can speed the aging process and hurt the pictures. Plus, if too many people handle the unprotected pictures, there is a greater chance of scratches or damage to photos.

- Store your pictures in a photo album or photo sleeves with acid-free protective sheets. These holders prevent yellowing, aging, and drying out of the pictures—so it won't look like your grandmother's photo album.

- Check www.exposuresonline.com to find these protective albums as well as specially treated acid-free photo frames that are designed to slow the aging process, keeping photos looking fresh.

- If you store-buy any albums or frames for gifts or for your personal use, check them out thoroughly to be sure they're free of PVC (polyvinyl chloride) and magnetic pages, both of which can age your pictures.

- Be careful where you store your photo albums; for example, never keep them in a damp basement or hot attic, as extreme temperatures will age your photos faster. And keep them away from electronic equipment, which also ages pictures. Keep them out of direct sunlight in your home, and make sure any children or grandchildren can't use the photo album as a coaster or "art project."

- Prepare for catastrophe. Since wedding photos and videos are the number-one thing most people say they'd attempt to retrieve from a burning house, you should store a copy of your wedding video, a duplicate wedding album, or a selection of wedding-day photos in a safe deposit box or a fireproof safe in your home.

- Insure wedding photographs and videotapes. Speak with an insurance expert about having these precious items added to your homeowner's policy for an extra nominal fee, and your policy will cover the costs if replacements are ever needed.

- Label your albums and videotapes or DVDs well and keep them separate from your other collections so no confusion occurs.

- When making copies of the wedding videotape for others, be careful with the master tape. For this task, it's best to order copies from the videographer or have an expert videotape editor use his or her editing system to make duplicates, rather than running the master tape through a recorder a dozen times for everyone on your list. Such overcopying can damage the quality of the master tape.

Disposable Cameras

You've seen plenty of those little disposable cameras at other weddings, the ones left on the guests' tables so that everyone at the party can take candid shots. It's a great idea, providing the couple with terrific shots of "moments" that are taking place around the room; the photographer can only shoot one thing at a time, after all! The happy newlyweds who were busy cutting the cake, getting a drink, or taking a walk for two minutes of alone time, will be thrilled to have pictures of these lovely moments. So don't skip this expense.

Getting Copies for Others

Here's another shopping list. Record who you'll get photos for, who gets wedding albums, and who gets copies of the wedding video. Use this chart to create your own gift list:

PERSON	INDIVIDUAL PICTURES	ALBUM	VIDEOTAPE
1.			
2.			
3.			
4.			
5.			
6.			
7.			
8.			
9.			
10.			

Remember that digital pictures taken on your camera can be uploaded into your home computer and processed and printed at sites like www.ofoto.com or through Target's Web site, among many others. For your candids, this could be the perfect, inexpensive method of development you need, plus it enables you to share your online "album" with others who may wish to order copies.

And then there's the option of posting photos to the couple's wedding Web site: It's a way for guests who couldn't make it to the wedding to see all the fun they missed, as well as the couple's big moment. Many couples post new photos to their site during the planning months, using their own cameras or those of friends, so make sure you remind the couple to complete their keepsake wedding Web site by putting a last photo and detailed journal entry or letter about how the wedding day went.

Looking Great in Photos and Video

Did I mention that the pictures and footage of the wedding day will be a lasting, *forever* keepsake. The way you look that day and the way you appear on tape will be saved for posterity . . . so you want to look great!

I don't mean that you have to lose twenty pounds and have your hair dyed, wear a designer dress, or strike poses like a supermodel. The key: watch your facial expressions. A videographer showed me some "outtakes" from the wedding he just shot. In that video, the mother of the groom was smiling and happy when she knew the camera was on her, but when she was in the background of shots not knowing she was being taped, she showed a different side. She was rolling her eyes, mocking family members, drinking way too much, and making a fool of herself. As my friend says, "The camera sees all." And it captures all forever. I'm sure the bride and groom were not pleased when they saw the mother's "performance."

Of course, you don't have a split personality or aren't phony, so I'm sure advising against rolling eyes at other guests isn't necessary, but remember that you're likely to be on camera when you least expect it. Carry yourself well, smile and be delightful, and don't bend over if you have a plunging neckline. Anything can be immortalized on film or tape.

Looking Better in Print

Here are a few pointers for looking your best on film:

- ❧ Keep your face shine-free. When the camera flash pops, it makes you look drenched or super-oily.

* Use a good foundation. Going too dark can make you look muddy and going too light can make you look like you're wearing a ghost-like white mask.

* Talk to your hairstylist before dyeing your hair. A great shade with highlights can look terrific on camera if it's done well. So make an appointment and perhaps even have your eyebrows darkened to frame your eyes better in print.

* Check your hairdo. Be sure your hairstyle suits you, and check the mirror in the ladies' room to see if you need a re-poufing or a taming of a wisp or curl.

* Watch your posture. You might not realize you're slouching, but the camera sees it.

* Slim down by standing differently. If you look at actresses and models, you'll see they know just how to stand to make themselves appear taller, thinner, curvier, and so on. It could be that just stepping out a little bit with your front foot or standing so that your hipbone is facing outward could shave ten pounds off how you look. Super-slim moms might want to jut out a hip to give themselves a more curvaceous appearance, or place a hand on one hip for the same effect. Practice in front of the mirror to see which stance makes you look like a Hollywood A-lister.

More beauty advice is provided in a later chapter . . . these tips are just to get you thinking about looking your best on film or tape.

CHAPTER 11

Riding in Style

LIMOUSINE . . . ROLLS-ROYCE . . . BENTLEY . . . a glass-encased, flower-strewn carriage pulled by a majestic white horse . . .

What kind of ride do the bride and groom want for their wedding day?

If they're going the traditional route, they might look no further than a gleaming white stretch limousine or black limousine, which will lend that celebrity panache and also look better in pictures with the dark car contrasting against the bride's white gown. To many couples, the search starts and ends with a limo.

However, since more brides and grooms are planning unique and personalized weddings, many favor unusual selections that are truly *them* over traditional options; they might be searching for an original, eye-catching way to make an entrance (and, later, their getaway). If so, here is another area where you can help.

Alternate Means of Transportation

These are some of the most stylish and unexpected modes of transportation that today's brides and grooms are arranging for their big day:

- **Boats**. From private yachts decorated with little white lights to gondolas, the seaside approach always thrills guests and makes for an unforgettable arrival and departure (as in "and they sailed off into the sunset").

- **Horses.** Especially for outdoor weddings in a wooded glen, a flower field, the grounds of a winery, or when the wedding will be held at a transformed, rustic barn, the romantic horseback ride is quite memorable.

- **Classic cars.** Aside from Rolls-Royces and antique Bentleys, brides and grooms are contacting their local classic-car clubs to see what kinds of impressive automobiles members rent out for special occasions. You could find a 1929 Packard or another ride your guests may have only seen in the Smithsonian or at a classic-car show. Remember, the cars you see at classic-car shows can sometimes be rented.

- **Testosterone rides.** Grooms love this one: a stretch Humvee or Navigator is a ride all the guys will love.

- **Convertibles.** Done well, you can neutralize any comparisons to the homecoming-day parade, where the Homecoming Queen and Princesses are slowly driven around the high school track by the kids who own convertibles. Today's convertibles, either rented or owned, are most easily decorated with flowers and signs that say JUST MARRIED.

- **Winter sports vehicles.** At some winter weddings, the bride and groom arrive via skis or snowmobiles, or they reach the summit ceremony site via the chairlift. This makes for fun pictures.

- **Take to the skies.** Whether in a hot-air balloon or a single-prop plane, all manner of brides and grooms across the country have arranged to soar to and from their weddings.

- **Trolley.** This option is picking up across the country—it's not just for San Francisco anymore. Rental agencies can send out decorated trolleys to drive the bride, groom, bridal parties, and parents to and from the wedding. Rice-a-Roni™ not included.

- **Subway.** City dwellers could have fun surprising their fellow straphangers by hopping onto the D train in full bridal attire. Also popular for residents of big cities and another fabulous photo opportunity: a yellow taxi or even a red tourist bus with an open top deck.

* **Party buses.** Visit any bridal expo and chances are you'll see one of these celebrity-worthy touring buses idling in the parking lot. These buses allow large groups, the bridal party and family members, to join the bride and groom in a party on wheels, complete with a great sound system, leather chairs, mood lighting, tables, and restrooms for a fun nightclub-on-wheels experience.

* **Horse and carriage.** This is among the most popular choices today. We're seeing a return to pure romance—the fairy-tale arrival for a bride. When booking a horse and carriage for the wedding day, be sure to ask the carriage operating company (found through a Web search or through the Carriage Operators of North America, www.cona.org) about the following covered carriages in case of uncooperative weather, traffic concerns regarding the route the horse will have to take, whether they'll need a permit for a police escort to lead and follow the carriage (some towns require it!), and if decorating the carriage with flowers and a sign is an option. Remember, the carriage-operating companies have the health and care of their horses to keep in mind, so they may refuse requests if they think the horse will be unsafe.

Creativity is running wild out there. Some of the most inventive approaches include arrivals and departures via the following: rollerblades, mountain bikes, ice skates, parachutes, scuba gear, Harley-Davidsons or other motorcycles, or even decorated wheelchairs when bride and/or groom use them. At lavish theme weddings, the bride might be carried in on a throne by a team of throne bearers, and at one wedding that made the news recently, the groom made his big entrance on the back of an elephant. The possibilities are almost endless.

Shopping for Cars

If you're in charge of transportation plans, you might need to scout out, research, interview, and hire rented cars for the big day. If this task falls to you, keep the following in mind while you look for the best agencies and car options out there:

- Always ask for referrals from people who have recently married or who often book limousines for business or personal use. The best way to tell the quality of service is through first-person experience, so consult with someone you trust.

- Another good source for finding the name of the best limousine or classic-car rental agency in your area is to talk with the concierge of a top hotel. Hotels often book limousine rides to the airport or to special meetings for their most important guests, so they might have a list of the best companies in town.

- Know that not too many limousine companies post their fees on their Web sites. Prices change according to season and demand (like high wedding season and prom season, the holidays, and holiday weekends) so be sure to ask for detailed price-package quotes.

- Don't go for the cheapest fare. You get what you pay for, and when it comes to getting the bride and groom to their ceremony and reception on time (and safely!) you want to make a good investment. So be prepared to spend a decent amount for this important service.

- Go to the agency to inspect the cars. You have to see the cars to make a good judgment. Some companies use newer cars that are in pristine condition, while other companies try to squeeze the last hundred miles out of a car they bought decades ago. Always ask for details on a car's age, and take a look for yourself. The cars should be in good condition, clean, and polished even when they are sitting in the lot.

- Check the car's interior. Be sure it is clean and doesn't smell of cigarette smoke, and has seats that are in good condition (not ripped), windows that work, and so on. Make sure there's plenty of legroom, considering that the bride's gown might be voluminous. She'll need to fit into the car while wearing it. Don't worry about sounding "fussy." Car companies expect you to want to check out the merchandise inside and out.

- Ask about the drivers. How much experience do they have? What kind of training do they get? (Drivers have to be specially licensed to drive limousines.) What will they wear? If it's appropriate to your plans, request that they wear black suits. These might sound like picky specifics, but you'll be happy you asked when the limo driver shows up looking snazzy and not like a sore thumb in a bright green windbreaker and a pair of shades.

- Ask about backup cars. Have it written into the contract that if a car breaks down, they'll send a replacement car immediately. Since we're talking about car emergencies, make sure the company you hire sends their drivers out not just with cell phones but also with two-way radios. As you probably know, cell-phone reception can be bad in some areas. The driver needs reliable access to his or her dispatcher in order to report any problems.

- Be clear about your requirements . . . the number of cars you'll need, how many hours you'll need them, where and when each will be needed. If you come prepared with this information, the task of booking cars can be accomplished much more efficiently.

- Read the contract and its fine print, and make sure the company has every detail spelled out in print. While you're at it, look for hidden terms like an automatic 18-percent gratuity added in for the driver. You don't want to tip him twice. And check for deposit information. You'll want to arrange a return of your deposit in case of mishaps or a change of plans.

❧ Ask about bridal specialties and extras. Some limousine companies will grant you the use of a red carpet that will be laid out in front of the car door for when the bride and groom return to the limousine after the ceremony concludes. Others will throw in free champagne placed on a champagne stand with crystal toasting flutes if a curbside toast is what the bride and groom want right after the ceremony. Others will stock the car's mini-bar with bottles of water, cans of soda, snacks, and so on. Some companies provide this sort of service for free as part of their five-hour wedding package, but others don't. This is an area where you might be able to negotiate a slight discount if you don't want the red carpet, champagne, or the chips-and-diet-soda stocked car. Ask ask about freebies and extras specifically.

Slipping Something into the Car

On the subject of extras and goodies, you could arrange to have a surprise waiting for them in the car upon their return after the ceremony or reception. Imagine their delight when they climb into the car to find a bouquet of roses from you for the bride, a thoughtful greeting card, a bottle of fine champagne that *you* selected, or a picnic basket filled with the makings of an intimate picnic for two: a half-dozen chocolate-covered strawberries, cubes of cheese, grapes, focaccia or breadsticks, even your own homemade brownies. The special surprise will be appreciated.

Free Ride

As mentioned earlier, you could get free transportation for your guests by using their hotel's shuttle bus. If the ceremony itself will take place at the hotel where the reception will be, and if the bride and groom have gotten a suite at the hotel for the night of the wedding—not to mention if you have a few volunteers who will drive the bride and groom in their own hot cars as their gift to the couple—you might not need to book any transportation. That could save thousands of dollars, so keep it in mind.

Anybody Need a Ride?

It's not just the bride and groom who may need a ride to the wedding and back home again. As a good host, you need to make sure that everyone has a reliable and safe ride wherever they need to be for the weekend of the wedding. Consider the following transportation needs your group might face, and then consider whether you will need to book a ride for each situation or enlist the help of a friendly bridal-party member or family friend to perform pickup and dropoff duties.

Before the Wedding

- Picking up the bride and groom or bridal party members from the airport or train station, if they will be coming in from out of town
- Picking up out-of-town guests who need a ride to their hotel when they arrive at the airport, or train or bus station
- Guest transportation to and from wedding weekend events, if their hotel does not provide shuttle service
- Guest transportation to the rehearsal
- Guest transportation to and from the rehearsal dinner
- Guest transportation to and from the bachelor and bachelorette's parties

- Safe rides home after any pre-wedding event where guests will be drinking. Take the keys. Call a cab. Safety first.

On the Wedding Morning

- Getting the bride and groom to where they will dress for the wedding
- Getting bridal party members and family to where they will prepare for the wedding
- Making a plan for all bridal-party members and family to have their cars ready for them after the wedding. This might include having them leave their cars at the reception site ahead of time and then shuttling in one mini-van to where they'll start their day.
- Getting the bride and her maids, and you and her mom, to the beauty salon on the morning of the wedding and then back to where you'll all prepare for the wedding
- Getting the bride and her parents to the ceremony site
- Getting the groom and his parents to the ceremony site
- Getting the bridal-party members to the ceremony site
- Getting special guests to the ceremony site (There's always the option of renting a limousine or classic car for grandparents, godparents, and other special guests as a treat for them, too!)

After the Ceremony

- Getting the bride and groom to a location where pictures will be taken after the ceremony
- Getting the bridal party to a location where pictures will be taken after the ceremony
- Getting all the parents and family members to a location where pictures will be taken after the ceremony

- Getting guests to the reception site
- Getting the bride and groom to the reception site
- Getting the bridal-party members to the reception site
- Getting the parents and special guests to the reception site

After the Reception

- Getting the bride and groom to their honeymoon suite *or* . . .
  Getting everyone to the after-party safely
- Getting the bridal party home safely
- Getting parents and special guests home safely
- Getting all guests home safely

The Next Day

- Getting guests, parents, the bridal party, and the bride and groom to a breakfast or other event that has been planned for the morning after the wedding
- Getting guests back to the airport, or train or bus station, for their return trips home

Special Rides

- Keep a designated driver available in case any emergency trips have to be made during the wedding (say, a run to the liquor store for more wine, or to a convenience store for ice or any forgotten ingredient)
- Handicapped or special-access guests could require specially outfitted vehicles

Arranging Airfare?

While it's not the responsibility of the bride's or groom's family to pay the airfare costs for faraway guests—although you may if you wish to—you can help them by arranging for a group discount on airplane tickets. While many airlines have group rates, check the American Airlines Web site for their new rates specifically for groups of wedding guests coming from the same area: www.aa.com.

* The ability for guests with kids to leave the festivities early if need be
* It's good to have the phone number of a cab company to transport any drunk guests after every wedding event. Keep that number with you.

Note here any additional special rides you or your group will have to plan:

* _____

* _____

* _____

* _____

Use the following worksheet to organize the pickup logistics. Give this sheet to the limousine or transportation company to get the wheels of organized pickup and dropoff in motion:

PICKUP AND DROPOFF DIRECTIONS

Car #1:

Date:

Time:

Street Address:

Phone number at street address or cell phone of person being picked up:

Name of person (people) being picked up:

Bring to this street address:

At this time:

Return pickup at this time and place:

Return to this street address:

Additional Notes:

Car #2:

Date:

Time:

Street Address:

Phone number at street address or cell phone of person being picked up:

Name of person (people) being picked up:

Bring to this street address:

At this time:

Return pickup at this time and place:

Return to this street address:

Additional Notes:

Make additional copies if you'll need more than two cars.

CHAPTER 12

A Place to Sleep

NO DOUBT AT LEAST a few guests will be coming from out of town. According to a recent survey in *WeddingBells* magazine, the average number of out-of-town guests attending the big event is a whopping *forty-one*. And you might even be one of them if you'll be traveling to the bride's hometown, to where the bride and groom live, or to a destination wedding. You'll need a comfortable, stylish place to stay, not just a room for the night, not just a bed and dresser and free HBO. It's going to be "home" for the wedding weekend, and you can make that "home" extra special and indulgent as well. Especially if one of the rooms you're planning to book is the bride and groom's wedding-night honeymoon suite!

Who Needs a Room?

In this space, record the names of the guests who are likely to need a hotel room for the wedding weekend:

_____

_____

_____

_____

_____

Don't forget, now that you have recorded all of your out-of-town guests' names, it's not just out-of-town guests who book rooms for weddings. Even local guests might decide to reserve a room near the reception site to keep their drive time to a minimum or to eliminate having to drive entirely if the reception will take place in the same hotel. Guests are wise not to drink and drive, especially after an all-day drinkfest like a wedding tends to be. They'll book a room to be safe. Also, groups of local guests may reserve a few rooms so that they can continue the party long into the night and "crash" right there.

This means arranging with your chosen hotel the approximate number of rooms you'll wish to include in your block for the wedding night or for the wedding weekend. Hotels offer blocks of rooms at discount rates when you book a wedding with them, and you can reserve blocks at hotels even if the wedding isn't taking place there. A sale is a sale. So talk to hotel booking managers to ask about group rates, and let your guests know the hotel names, addresses, phone numbers, and Web sites—along with your block's code number or the name the rooms are listed under—so that they can get your group discount.

Notice I said "hotels." As mentioned earlier, it's smart to set up blocks at several different hotels, to allow for your guests' choice of scale and location. Some might prefer to stay closer to the reception site; some won't mind traveling a bit farther to stay at a nicer hotel.

Selecting Hotels

It's not just about location, it's about quality of service. You want your guests to be comfortable and in a beautiful room, well taken care of, and perhaps pampered with a few extra indulgences. You can't beat a hotel where the bed is turned down for you, a chocolate is placed on your pillow, and a luxurious robe is waiting for you in the bathroom.

I spoke with recent marrying couples and their families about their "hotel hunts" and heard the following stories:

> *"We're lucky we went upstairs to see the rooms at a well-known resort chain with a big name. At this particular hotel, the rooms were very small, the bed saggy, and the view would have been*

of the parking lot. And we could hear everything from the hotel's bar down below. We scratched that one off our list."

—Dianne and Roger

"The events manager started showing us the more business-class rooms, but we asked her to show us the better rooms, ones with terraces and great views. Those were the rooms we wanted, the ones we saw on their Web site. She told us it would cost extra to reserve those kinds of rooms, which we gladly paid extra for. We wanted our guests to have great rooms, not crappy rooms at a discount." —Ellen and Charles

"Since our wedding was taking place in the off season, the hotel offered us their suites rather than their regular rooms for the regular-room price. We toured them and loved them. Our guests loved them too." —Renee and Taylor

Amenities

Obviously, the rooms you're looking at need to be clean, attractive, in good condition, with comfortable beds and modern décor. But another important factor is the hotel itself and the amenities it provides. After all, for many of your guests, this might be their vacation, and it could be that the events of the wedding weekend have them staying at the hotel for two to three nights. The more the hotel or resort offers, the better. You're placing your guests where they'll have a great time.

The amenities to look for at the most ideal of locations include the following:

- **Several different kinds of eateries.** A restaurant, a lounge or bar, even a sports bar would be great places for your guests to socialize.

- **Spa offerings.** Many hotels and resorts have gyms, salons, spa treatments, saunas . . . the works. Your guests will love having the opportunity to get their workouts in or get a massage during the schedule downtime in the wedding weekend.

- **Sporting facilities,** like access to nearby tennis clubs and golf courses, even horseback riding.

- **Pools and Jacuzzis.** Everyone from families to singles and your senior guests might love taking a morning swim or hanging out by the pool during a hot afternoon.

- **Room service.** Make sure you ask. Some hotels do not have room service, or they stop serving at 10 P.M. After the reception, your guests might love to order some snacks or sodas.

- **Internet access.** Whether it's a port in the room or a computer lounge, your guests will appreciate being able to log on to check messages or quickly send in that emergency message to work.

- **Kids' activities.** Your hotel might have a staff of daycare workers with planned activities to keep the children entertained. They can only spend so much time in an arcade, and with the widespread popularity of X-Box and Playstations, they might look at the ancient Ms. Pac Man in the run-down arcade and not know what it is.

- **Touring opportunities.** The hotel's concierge will be able to offer information if not tickets to local shows and points of interest. If the wedding location is in a historic town, planned outings and walking tours through the chic streets could be a fun for your guests.

Of course, there's much more that a hotel or resort can offer, including a prime spot on the beach, surfing lessons, and five-star cuisine in addition to that great snack bar by the pool. Keeping in mind the vacation element, be sure the hotel you choose has plenty to offer your guests . . . and then leave them time to enjoy it during the weekend.

Aside from Hotels

You might want to include some other places to stay in your accommodation search. One of the most popular options, especially when the location of the wedding brings you all to wine country or a beach where such things are plentiful

Guests' Special Needs

Make sure guests with special needs get their special needs met. No, I don't mean your alcoholic uncle who wants a minibar full of Stoli or your dog of a nephew who wants female company. By this, I mean handicapped access to rooms or bungalows, nonsmoking rooms or smoking rooms, rooms with cribs, and a special request that many guests make: rooms only on the eighth floor or lower. Some guests are uncomfortable with high-floor rooms in the event of a fire or other emergency. Fire truck ladders can reach all windows up to and including the eighth floor of a building. Assuring guests with this particular need that they can stay on lower floors can assuage their fears. Again, it sounds picky, but you might be surprised at people's wishes.

(and gorgeous and charming!) is the bed-and-breakfast. Couples love reserving B&Bs for their guests, as many say such an establishment is warm and cozy, gives their guests a "home" to socialize in, and breakfast always is the hit of the day. Not to mention that many of the better B&Bs provide discount tickets to local attractions like wine tours, hot-air balloon rides, and bike rentals . . . and many are located in terrific tourist areas where antique shops, quaint eateries, outlet shopping centers, and historic homes are plentiful. For these couples, staying at a resort is too much like the average family's typical summer vacation. Staying at a B&B is unique, which is just what they're looking for. Again, visit several and choose your favorite.

Some couples rent houses, such as those by a lake, on oceanfront property, or by a ski resort, where their guests will stay for the wedding weekend. If you've ever seen the available beach- or ski-house rentals out there, you know that some come with pools, Jacuzzis, spiral staircases, suites and lofts, grand kitchens, libraries with fireplaces, entertainment centers, even screening rooms and wine cellars. It all depends on your budget, but you might find that, rather than paying for fifteen hotel rooms for the weekend, spending $1,000 or $2,000 for a weekend at such a house is a savings. It's something to explore.

And, of course, there's always inviting select out-of-town guests to stay at your house. It makes sense, and you might enjoy the opportunity to host your favorite relatives and friends for the weekend. You might love the chance to show off your home and entertain at your place. I'm not going to deter you, but keep in mind that things are likely to be very hectic on the weekend of the wedding. It might be a bit too stressful to have guests in the house, especially if your guests are a bit demanding or not aware that you're busy. Think about it and see if you can handle having extra housework and having to wait for the shower to be available. It's up to you and how particular you are, and how well you handle so much extra activity underfoot. Many parents end up regretting opening up their homes to relatives and their kids . . . it was more work than they expected, and the last thing they needed on a very busy weekend.

A Room for the Couple

As the mother of the groom, one of the many special things you might like to do to treat the bride and groom with extra loving care is to reserve a special suite for their first night as husband and wife. Sending them on their way in high style could be a gift from you.

Check out not only the honeymoon suite but the presidential suite, the best room in the house. These rooms can be on the top floor with a sweeping view of the cityscape, a terrace large enough for outdoor dining, a shower with a half-dozen shower heads, a king-size bed, décor that's been featured in *Architectural Digest*, a fireplace, and personal service by a first-class staff of butlers and maids. Silk robes and slippers, a canopy bed, a Jacuzzi in the room—just pure indulgence. They're worth it.

Or, you could turn a regular hotel room into something very special by arranging for the delivery of flowers, a bottle of champagne, a pre-ordered room-service feast for a post-midnight snack, chocolate-covered strawberries, or a fruit platter. You might even have the bed covered in rose petals. With permission from the hotel, you can set the room up with safe, glass-enclosed candles, and a special gift awaiting them on their arrival (like the news that you've also arranged for a limousine to take them from the airport to their resort when they arrive at their honeymoon locale).

Isn't it a little bit weird for me to be setting up a palace of seduction for my *son?*, you might ask. It would be if you were setting up the room as if for a bachelor party. Your goal is to create a romantic atmosphere, something they'll both remember and be grateful for. If you feel strange about surprising them like this, talk to your son and ask how he'd feel if you arranged for the honeymoon suite. It could then be a surprise for the bride, or you might find out that this arrangement is something he's already been working on to surprise his new bride. If so, just send a little something for their romantic evening.

If you don't want to arrange for a honeymoon-suite surprise for the night of the wedding, perhaps arrange for some royal treatment for the morning after. Order and pick up the tab for an elaborate breakfast to be delivered to the couple's room in the morning: eggs Benedict, crêpes, fruit, bagels with cream cheese and lox, bacon and sausage, mimosas, and coffee. This early-morning treat gives the couple a romantic breakfast in bed and a true feast to start off their first full day as husband and wife.

Your Lodging

Hey, who says the bride and groom are the only ones who deserve five-star service for their wedding-night accommodations? Why not book a suite and the royal treatment for yourselves as well?

You've given your all to help plan the wedding, you may have paid for a huge chunk of it, and you have plenty to celebrate as well! Your son is a married man, jetting off happily with the love of his life to Bora Bora or Belize. As the proud parents, you deserve to indulge!

Just don't stay next door to the happy couple, okay?

Choose a great suite or hotel room for yourselves, and go the extra mile. Order up room service just for the two of you, buy a great set of lingerie to surprise and seduce your partner, bring along romantic music and massage oils, get those chocolate-covered strawberries and sprinkle those rose petals on the bed. In the morning, order up that great breakfast in bed, sip your mimosas, and enjoy your first full day as parents of a married man and your new daughter-in-law.

As for the wedding breakfast you might have planned for all of your guests before their departure the morning after the wedding, you can still offer that. Enjoy that breakfast buffet with all of your loved ones, look at their digital pictures from the wedding, kiss the bride and groom good-bye and wave farewell as the shuttle takes them to the airport; then the two of you can go to your spa appointments, your tee time, or just back to your room. Once more, let the celebrations begin!

PART THREE

*All About
the Reception*

CHAPTER 13

A Beautiful Room

THINK BACK TO the last wedding you attended. Wasn't it wonderful when you walked into the reception ballroom and got your first glimpse of the breathtaking floral centerpieces, flickering candles, sparkling crystal glasses on the tables, and the spotlights on the band in their tuxedos and gowns? The tables were set like something right out of the pages of a magazine. You could smell the gardenia-scented candles. The roses in the centerpieces still glittered with dew and had bloomed to perfection. The ambiance of a beautifully designed ballroom takes you into another world—you just know a special evening is about to begin.

If you're involved in choosing the décor for your son's wedding, you get to be a part of creating a magical, ethereal setting for the reception as well. You get to sit before the blank canvas that is a plain, old ballroom—tables, chairs, walls, and floor—and help make the decisions that will transform it into something more ravishing than you've ever seen before. All to create the wedding scene your son and his bride dream about.

In this chapter, you'll start considering ideas for the reception décor, and you'll read about some of the latest, hottest trends in the wedding realm straight from the world of celebrity movie premieres, Fortune 500–company galas, the Oscars, and the Golden Globes. You've seen the gold-dusted party rooms on "Entertainment Tonight," "Extra," and E! Television plus more than a few celebrity weddings in primetime, and you'll be thrilled to know that the wedding industry is now taking those top-dollar ideas ($750,000 for flowers at a recent celebrity wedding!) and making them available at realistic prices for the real-world bride and groom. The couple should feel like celebrities for the day, they should get the royal treatment, and every one of those extravagant decorating concepts can be arranged for them within a budget.

Centerpieces

Before we start talking about the size and content of floral centerpieces, it's a good idea to start thinking about other places you can put them. Besides centering each of the guests' tables with a beautiful arrangement, you can also choose to place one . . .

- On the piano during the cocktail hour, or on the piano for the reception entertainment
- On the gift table
- On the sign-in table where the guests' place cards will be arranged and the guestbook will be set up
- On the buffet tables or serving station
- On windowsills in the reception room, to bring the décor effect outward
- On pedestals in "blank spots" of the room: corners, balconies, in front of windows that have no windowsills
- In the hallway leading to the reception room
- In restrooms, which is always a nice touch, especially in the ladies' room
- On coffee tables and end tables in cocktail-hour sitting rooms
- On the bar
- On the dessert table

Depending on your budget, you can place even small arrangements here and there to bring the full floral effect to the reception, cocktail, and after-party areas.

And keep in mind that the following ideas work for any wedding weekend event, from the rehearsal dinner to the brunch the morning after the wedding.

Floral Centerpieces

You've seen them on the covers and within the pages of wedding magazines and in design books at florists' studios: gorgeous masses of white roses, gardenias, lilies of the valley; pastel shades of pink with bright mauves and greens so bright you'd swear they were picked from right outside. Ranunculus and tight clusters of peonies with gently rippled edges.

It's no wonder your guests really want to win the centerpiece to take home at the end of the evening!

Centerpieces have changed markedly in the past few years. First they were enormous, filling the centers of tables with such bounty that guests couldn't see past them. Then they were elevated onto high pedestals, still enormous and sprawling. Then, they got smaller: tight clusters of blooms set low in glass bowls to facilitate sight and conversation among guests. And now they're getting bigger again, once more going up on those high crystal, silver, or Lucite pedestals.

In a nutshell, any of these choices work . . . whether you're going oversized with flower arrangements or keeping them small, simple, streamlined, and elegant. It all depends on the look the couple wants.

In choosing individual flowers and groupings for centerpieces, know that florists can do anything you ask, from very bridal to more colorful and modern. Couples today are requesting a range of "looks," from those traditional, all-white floral arrangements to bright groupings with color as the main attraction. Bright reds, purples and lavenders, sage greens mixed with white (such as with green calla lilies and lilies of the valley). So ask your floral designer to show many possibilities before you choose. And don't forget that you can bring in a photo or several photos to ask the stylist to copy the elements you like.

If you're going small, look at the classy, simple line of little round bud vases with a single bloom in each, all clustered in the center of a round table or arranged in a line on a longer table.

There also is the lovely look of a round glass bowl filled with water and holding a single, dramatic gardenia or lotus flower—or a larger glass bowl holding three or four of these eyecatching flowers.

Flowers and More

One trend that's picking up in the floral-centerpiece department is mixing a selection of flowers with *other items* in the centerpiece. From flowering branches to give more height and reach to a smaller, more compact floral arrangement with inserted glossy fresh fruit or sugar-glazed fruits (brushed with egg white and dusted with sugar to give that ice-crystal look you've seen), it's all about color, texture, and elements of nature.

One gorgeous look that belies its low cost is the glass bowl holding cut flowers, but filled at the bottom with cranberries. The glass bowl of cranberries gives a pop of color, which can contrast with or match the color of the flowers. Think about what can be placed in the bowl to create a visual impact: small lemons, berries, colored stones, shells, and so on.

No Flowers at All!

Another idea for centerpieces is to skip the floral arrangement and decorate guest tables with something useful, like a lovely basket with a selection of warm gourmet breads, rolls, and breadsticks and surrounded by cups of spreads, olive oil, tapenade, or garlic butter. The centerpiece—literally beautiful enough to eat—becomes part of the meal.

Or center the table with something unique, like a glass bowl filled with sand and seashells, or a basket of pine cones and evergreen shoots, with some holly leaves to match a holiday wedding's theme. At some beach weddings, couples are centering their tables with fishbowls containing live or windup goldfish with color coordinated stones at the bottom.

At one garden wedding, the couple used long, family-style tables and the bride's father built long, narrow planters which were then filled with potting soil and grass seed. By the time the wedding came around, they used these grassy planters as centerpieces, which gave the natural look they wanted.

At autumn weddings, you might center the table with a pumpkin (carved or not) and some unique speckled gourds of varying sizes.

At winter weddings, fill a crystal serving platter with a display of glass holiday ornaments in a color that works with the wedding's hues. Or, clear glass ornaments inscribed with silver designs or lettering gives an extra bit of sparkle without being overbearing. Look through the offerings in holiday ornaments just after the winter holidays, when everything could be sold for 50- to 75-percent off! Even better!

And use plenty of framed family portraits, wedding pictures—special family moments captured on film to share with all of your guests.

Garlands and Greens

Many of today's couples are looking for ways to work more greenery into their weddings. From garlands of evergreen branches to trailing ivy, topiaries, and feather-light ferns, they want to bring in the green.

One new trend in greenery display is using potted trees to completely transform a room. These run the gamut from tropical trees to ficus, evergreens to flowering trees. One couple rented a dozen kumquat trees for a truly unique look. The delicate yellow-orange of the growing kumquats matched their yellow-orange wedding color scheme, and the trees were the perfect accessory to their room!

Be sure to ask your floral designer about the many ways you can use more greenery in your décor. Done well—and as an inexpensive option—you can triple the effect of the décor without increasing your budget.

Candles

It wouldn't be a wedding without candles, right? Flickering, warm candlelight—particularly in a dimmed room—provides lovely, romantic ambiance, an intimate setting, and elegance. So consider the following types of candles for the look that's perfect for each area of your reception locale:

* Large pillar candles with three wicks, of varying heights
* Regular pillar candles of varying heights

- Multicolor pillar candles
- Pillar candles that contain embedded items, like dried fruits, cranberries, stones, flowers, seashells
- Votive candles
- Taper candles in stand-alone candleholders
- Taper candles in candelabras
- Taper candles inserted into centerpiece arrangements

The world of candle design knows no limits, and you can find candles in any shape, size, color, or scent. Start your search at www.illuminations.com, a favorite source of mine, or visit your local Pier 1 Imports, craft shop, even home-decorating stores for options.

A mixture of candle shapes and sizes brings a zing to your centerpieces; for instance, center a three-wick pillar candle, and then surround it with matching votives in pretty glass holders. Or choose a triangular candle or pyramid-shaped candle for the table centerpieces. Mix solids and multicolors, or alternate color schemes among your tables, using blush pink pillars and votives at every other table and deeper rose colors at the rest.

And finally, for a great, inexpensive effect you can sprinkle flower petals on each tablecloth around the candles.

Always use safe votive candles or candleholders, including hurricane lamps, when candles might be anywhere near a curtain, foliage, or in guests' way (such as on a buffet table). Safety always comes first, when you're using candles as a decorative element, so be sure to take extra precautions.

Linens

Tablecloths, napkins, slipcovers, curtains . . . that's another area where reception décor has come of age, and there are plenty of designer linen rental companies out there to prove the trend. I know of two recent fashion institute graduates who started their own business in the table-linen industry who now work with the top

> ### Mirror Image
>
> You can magnify and multiply the look of your candles by placing them on mirrored platters, which reflect the candlelight and give your centerpiece a more finished look.

national wedding coordinators. Forget designing dresses, the real opportunities for success are in tablecloths!

And what an opportunity you'll have when you start looking through the marvelous selection of linens for rent out there. Silk dupioni, brocades, laces—in any color from pastels to brights, perhaps even overlaid with sheers with attached crystals.

Today's tables and chairs have shine, pattern, texture, and *personality*. So skip that selection of polyester tablecloths the reception site hands you, those same twelve colors they've been offering for decades—and try something a little different.

Pay particular attention to chair slipcovers, which allow you to turn rented chairs into works of art. Use either straight fabric slipcovers tied at the base, or even new stretchy fabrics that conform to the chair's shape. Add tassels and hooks for attaching little floral nosegays to the backs of chairs—for a special touch that adds extra glamour to the room. It's the little things like this that complete the transformation.

On buffet tables and the gift table, look for runners in contrasting colors, sheers, and monochromatic colors with extra shine to set them apart. For the cake table, look at fabrics that are studded with crystals or pearls, or a color of fabric that coordinates with the shades of the flowers used to decorate the cake.

Whether you're looking for a soft touch of color or want to go fully Moroccan with oranges, reds, yellows, and burnt umbers . . . bright reds . . . deep purples . . . the way to provide a dramatic color scheme for the room is through linens.

Chopsticks by Design

At receptions where Asian food will be served—a hot trend now—couples are offering their guests silverware *and* artistic, high-quality chopsticks. And not those wooden ones you get with takeout Chinese food. Instead, they are authentic with painted motifs or a pearlized sheen—just the artistic touch for the tables.

Table Settings

Each table can be a work of art. With the right choices of china, crystal, and stemware, a gorgeously set table can depict both the couple's wedding style and their personalities. The site might offer its own selection of fine bone china in a range of designer styles from simple and elegant white with silver rims to floral designs, plus their own range of silverware and stemware in lovely designs, but you can go one step further and rent the latest styles.

You can look at bridal-friendly designs in florals or Victorian swirls, Tiffany place settings, and understated looks, or you can go with color. It's easy to dress up elegant white or cream-colored place settings with a colored charger set beneath them; for example, a hunter green charger brings out the white in the setting and also plays up the green of the centerpiece. These days, it's especially popular to jazz up table settings with red, so that could mean lipstick red chargers, even red water goblets.

Look at different shapes for plates, such as squares or rectangles, all of which are plentiful in the rental field. Check out sushi platters and deep, oversize pasta bowls to allow for a more interesting presentation for that slab of salmon over linguine or tortellini alfredo. Bright colors can further add to the décor of the table, so don't stop at wedding-specific designs. Ask your rental agent to show you the works.

Check out the offerings in glassware, too, from martini glasses to red and white wineglasses, snifters, and footed water glasses. Some come with colored stems, some with colored rims, and all coordinate into masterfully designed tabletops.

As for tableware, the designs are also endless. Pay attention to sizes and designs, laser-swirled accents on handles, and colored handles. Know your shrimp fork from your salad fork and dress up the table accordingly.

Lighting

Ask any wedding coordinator—and the events producers for the post-Oscars gala—to name the one thing that best sets the mood and tone of a reception room, and they'll say great lighting. From pinlights set above each table to shine down on the centerpieces, to colored lighting, soft lights aimed at the gift table, shaded lights spotlighting the buffet table, and laser lights when the party gets hopping . . . all of these can be arranged by a lighting specialist.

That's right, another professional wedding expert to hire, but the effects will be worth it. No more dimmer switches on a room's standard overhead lights. Now, experts can place spotlights to make the cake even more of a focal point in the room; strategic uplights in corners to aim up the walls and give extra effect to any curtains or fabric swags, artwork, or window detailing; and colored lights to make the dance floor look like a rippling blue sea (ever danced on water before?). They also can create moving starburst light effects that make the dance floor come alive before anyone has ever set foot on it.

Special effects can be light-driven, as in the case of projection lights or "gobo" lights that use a specially designed laser-cut disc to project an image or words onto walls, the ceiling, the dance floor, tent sides, lawns, and even pool surfaces. You might have the couple's names projected onto the dance floor, or turn plain tent walls into a flower-filled field. One wedding designer told me she created a Moroccan rug design and had that projected onto the surface of a swimming pool. Lasers make the dancing hours into a nightclub scene, and new special-effects lasers can create virtual fireworks on almost any surface.

Outside the reception area, lighting can emphasize fountains, pools, ponds, trees and gardens, and the dramatic architecture of the building.

Strings of white fairy lights or twinkle lights can line the banisters of a stair-way, the railing of a wraparound porch, the mast of a yacht, and the highest branches of trees à la the famous look at New York City's Tavern on the Green. Strings of fairy lights can be colored or strung to look like icicles for a winter wedding, and you can even purchase novelty lights such as Chinese lanterns and other quirky shapes like chili peppers or golf balls to fit with your wedding's theme.

Light should also be used for safety, so check out lighting needs for outdoor walkways, parking areas, and terraces that will be used during the party.

Seating

In addition to the chairs for the ceremony and reception, usually standard-fare folding chairs, you can arrange additional seating with mingling in mind. During the cocktail party, the poolside reception, the after-party, and even on outdoor terraces during the reception, you can set up any or all of the following to make your guests comfortable:

- **Couches.** That's right, couches—but not your usual three-seaters or loveseats. Now, you can get Victorian couches, overstuffed couches, and backless couches in color-coordinated hues.
- **Adirondack chairs.** For outdoor weddings or outdoor cocktail parties, group some of these open-air chairs for mingling time.
- **Chair groupings.** Set some comfy chairs by the fireplace, or out on a terrace, for "talk stations" where guests might congregate.

Tables

The new look in reception décor calls for a change in shape. It's no longer just round eight-to-ten-seat tables arranged for the guests. Consider the following options as you assess the space you're using, your guest head count, and how you want to group your guests so they have a better time. Where they're seated, and with whom, does make a difference:

Where *Shouldn't* You Have Chairs?

At the bar. You don't want guests parking themselves at the bar for one drink after another, and you don't want anyone blocking other guests' access to that great wine you're serving. So ask the site to remove the barstools before the party begins.

* Long, family-style tables for eighteen to twenty
* Square eight- to ten-seat tables, which experts say facilitate conversation much better than round tables
* A mixture of table shapes: round, rectangular, square
* A specially shaped table where parents and grandparents can sit together, such as a longer rectangular table, while all other guests sit at circular tables. This is a way for both sets of parents and grandparents to be at Table Number One and show familial unity. Some couples make this tablecloth white to match theirs at the head table, while guests' tablecloths are colored.
* And, of course, the sweetheart table for the bride and groom, who can sit together and have a few moments alone during the reception

Extra-Special Effects

Borrowing once again from celebrity special events, it's the effects that will have everyone talking at your wedding. You can arrange for more complex options: laser shows, fireworks, and plasma-screen TVs playing a specially produced DVD of family photos, or a video of the bride and groom showing images of them as children and teenagers (just like montages at the Oscars!). You can even rent special machines that create snowfall in the room. The magical solution used to create this snow evaporates before it hits the ground. Check with rental agencies for these special effects, fireworks agencies for the permits and safety standards you'll need to adhere to (as well as whether fireworks or any pyrotechnics are legal in your state), and the site's managers before you plan for any special effects in the first place.

Using the Site's Decorative Elements

Of course the site is chosen for its beauty and charm, its function, and its proximity to the ceremony site, but if you're wise you'll choose it for its decorative possibilities. Some sites, for example, have floor-to-ceiling windows overlooking the ocean, providing an unforgettable sunset lightshow.

At a winter resort, there might be a vista of snow-covered mountains and also the effect of nighttime skiers coming down the mountain with lanterns or flashlights.

At the beach, you can hire sand-sculpture artists to create enormous sandcastles, or other sand structures for guests to admire at the party.

Gazebos on the grounds of an estate can be decorated with floral garlands, with a comfy bench set in the middle of it. Guests will certainly want their pictures taken there.

Fireplaces on the site can be lit, balconies can be open for access and again set with flowers, candles, and private seating, and wine cellars can be lit with sconces and set with centerpieces and platters of cheese and crackers for tasting.

Look at the site to see what it can offer, not just for what you can arrange. The result will be the coming together of many points of beauty, in a one-of-a-kind setting.

CHAPTER 14

Everything Is Delicious!

As the mom, you might be the first person the bride and groom come to for help creating their menus. And notice I said menus, since there are more events to feed people at than just the reception dinner. You'll have wedding-weekend events, brunches, cocktail parties, perhaps even a shower at which to feed your guests. This section will start you thinking about the most delectable, *unique*, and elegant food and drink choices for every food event. Feel free to circle or highlight the choices here that tempt your taste buds, and bring these pages to the caterer to illustrate your wishes.

Choosing Your Style

For each event—cocktail party, reception, brunches, breakfasts, barbecues, wine-and-cheese parties—you'll need to start by selecting a presentation *style*:

- Buffet
- Passed items served by waiters
- Food stations in several different areas throughout the room. (These can be either freestanding stations where guests help themselves or "action stations" where a chef or attendant creates dishes or ladles out servings.)

- Sit-down meal, served by waiters
- Sit-down meal, family style, where all dishes are on the table and passed by guests
- Sit-down meal with "Russian service": Waiters fill each individual guest's plate from larger platters of food
- Traveling event where food stations and food servers are located in different rooms, perhaps with different themes and different serving styles

Establishing the style of serving for any event will in part dictate the food choices. The caterer will need this information so that he or she can plan not just the menu but the timing of servings so, for example, all hot passed hors d'oeuvres will be hot when served. And you, too, can better envision which menu choices you'd like to see on your elaborate buffet table or on those shiny silver platters being presented to the guests.

Foods in Season

Just like flowers, certain foods are "in season" and "out of season" at specific times of the year. That means their availability is variable, and prices may fluctuate. Ask your caterer which seafoods, as well as certain meats and specialty game, are going to be at their peak at the time of your wedding. Keep in mind that the market for seafood especially can often be unpredictable, as the various weather and ecological conditions will drastically affect whether the lobster fishermen and clam diggers have had a good week. Your caterer, like many restaurants, might hold off on quoting a price for the seafood bar you want until the market rates are known.

Finding a Caterer

Consider the caterer you hire as the "make or break" decision for the success of the entire wedding. If the food isn't terrific—the guests are grimacing at the soggy shrimp and joking among themselves that they should order out for pizza—that's what they'll remember. It doesn't matter how lovely the bride looks or how beautifully decorated the room is. If the food is subpar, so is the wedding. That's an awful thing for the bride and groom to bear. So remind them of this fact, and put your all into finding, interviewing, and auditioning caterers to find the best chef in town.

What are the qualities of a terrific caterer? Expertise and skill in food preparation, of course, but also creativity. Like an artist mixing colors or to create something breathtaking in the combinations, so, too, should your chef be able to take dishes and turn them into masterpieces.

First ask for referrals. Talk to anyone you know who has been married recently, or who has planned events for corporations and charities, for references to the best caterers with whom they've worked recently. People in the know can tell you who got raves. Next, check with culinary associations to make sure any caterers you have in mind are professionally trained, with credentials. The best of the best out there can claim anywhere from one to five professional memberships, and their profiles on expert-locator sites can even tell you the many awards the caterer has won or major magazines the caterer has been featured in.

This is *not* the place to skimp. *You get what you pay for* is not a regret you want the couple to have after their wedding. So invest well, go for the best, and be willing to pay extra for the special touches that will make the food at the event delicious and impressive.

Tastings

When you have your list of prospective caterers in hand, interview them in person. Schedule a "tasting," where the caterer will show you not just the list of menu options he or she can create for the wedding, but you'll be able to try a wide array of them. Platters will be set in front of you with sample-size portions of the chef's creations, from the scampi to the potato-crusted salmon and the chocolate dessert mousse. Take notes as you taste, especially if you will be going for tastings at several different caterers' offices (which you most definitely should!). Don't rely on memory alone. It will serve you well at decision time if you can flip open your notebook and see that you actually said "The Chateaubriand just melted in my mouth!"

Besides the Appetizers, How's Your Attitude?

Remember, you're not just interviewing caterers for the tenderness of their filet mignon or the creaminess of their crème brulée, but also for their personalities! These masters of culinary genius must be professional, open to your questions and suggestions, and willing to explain to you in a courteous manner that a certain wine doesn't go with a certain dish or that your choice of dressing won't hold up well on a hot summer day. The caterer must be personable, welcoming, open-minded, and pleasant to deal with. He or she must understand that you're trying to make important decisions, that you're depending on him or her for guidance. In every industry, you'll find a few snobs and people who are rude because they're overwhelmed with work, but you don't want to hire anyone who treats you with anything less than professional courtesy. If the vibe is bad, move on to the next candidate. There is plenty of competition.

Mothers of the groom and bride are often invited to these tastings, even when the bride and groom are paying for the wedding themselves, to give reliable second opinions. You know food quality, after all, and the couple may need you to be the tiebreaker between two top-notch caterers.

In addition, there's a safety factor. Since it's food and drink you're planning to give your guests, you must make sure the caterer is licensed and insured, and that their kitchens have been recently inspected and are clean and up to safety standards. This is very important, and it's a step too many people skip. They just assume a professional caterer is going to have a clean workspace, and they don't bother to look. Look! If the caterer won't allow you in the kitchen, move on. You have a right to judge where your guests' food will be prepared.

The same goes if you're hiring a caterer to cook on-site, such as using portable ovens or refrigerator units for your outdoor wedding. Search for details, and ask about food safety.

You can learn a lot about a caterer's concern for food safety by asking a few questions about choosing menu selections when the weather will be hot. A knowledgeable caterer will recite the many rules he or she keeps in mind, such as not leaving the cake out in warm weather but rather bringing it out of the refrigerator just before it's being served. You'll hear about how the caterer will set any salad dressings in a carved-out block of ice or in a platter of ice chips. Some menu choices may be nixed if the caterer doesn't think they can be safely served at your hot-weather wedding.

"We were very impressed with our caterer's concern about our guests' safety. We wanted a cheese platter for our cocktail party, and that extra order would have put a nice chunk of change in the caterer's pocket. But she told us that cheese platters are too hard to keep cold enough when they're set out for a three-hour event and that she didn't want anyone getting sick, especially pregnant guests. She told us about a case of listeria that hit a conference's guests because cheeses weren't kept cold; several people almost died. We appreciated her honesty and skipped the cheese platter." —Toni, recent bride

"We had asked for a raw seafood bar, knowing that other friends of ours had oysters and clams on the half shell at their weddings. Our caterer encouraged us to skip the raw seafood bar for safety reasons and instead be a bit more original with a steamed seafood bar that, as it turned out, way more of our guests loved!"
—Wendy and Al, recently married

Finally, you'll want to make sure the caterer can do the kinds of dishes you want at the wedding. Ask if she has a Latin-inspired menu or if she can make pierogis for your ethnic wedding. See if she has a repertoire in the food themes you're after to find the perfect chef and creator of the best menu possible.

When the Caterer Comes with the Site

Some reception locations stipulate the use of their on-site caterer, or you may only get to choose from a list of three approved caterers. Indeed, the site of the wedding may very well prescribe who you can hire, so consider that when you're considering your site, and interview these "approved" chefs as you would any other, complete with tastings.

Be sure your caterer can do his or her job at the site you've chosen. She might not do outdoor weddings where she has to prepare the meal in a tent, or she might not be able to fit her oversize platters into the smaller oven at an estate home. Always make sure you disclose your chosen location when you start talking to caterers.

Do It Yourself?

In some areas of the country, and in some religious or cultural circles, all of the food for the wedding is made not by a caterer but by hand. The women of the families get together for an evening and make all of the appetizers, salads, entrées, and desserts. Groups of relatives and friends sit around the dining room table and make spanakopita, spring rolls, or antipasto salads as they chat and gossip in a celebratory mood. Not to be gender-biased, the men are also well inclined to pitch in with the cooking and prep work. This sort of preparation for the wedding is sometimes a party in itself.

Or, relatives and friends might offer to bring their renowned lasagne, suckling pig, marinated artichokes, apple strudel, and the like as a pitch-in for the wedding party.

If this option appeals to you, just accept the kindhearted help of your loved ones, and count this prep party as among the many great memories built around the wedding. Don't take on more than you can handle by volunteering to do a lot of cooking for the wedding. Eager-to-help moms often start out with good intentions as they volunteer to make the hors d'oeuvres but then find themselves frantically baking all night, facing the challenge of preparing food for two hundred guests. At any other time, they'd be fine with it. But with the countdown to the wedding bringing about many additional details that need to be handled, time compresses, and it's easy to become overwhelmed. Keep contributions within a reasonable range, and be sure you can handle all you're volunteering to do.

Many mothers who go the do-it-yourself route for the wedding say, after the fact, that they wished they had hired a caterer. If you foresee this kind of pressure for yourself, it's enough to contribute to the wedding by making a few dishes or one showstopping dessert. That way, a dish by the mother of the groom is still a noteworthy part of the meal that guests will appreciate just as much as if you'd made everything yourself.

Menu Selection Ideas

Original Choices

Caterers love it when you're willing to veer away from the usual menu choices: unique chicken dishes, fish other than salmon, and meats other than filet mignon. They're food artists, and they appreciate getting the opportunity to go beyond standard fare and flexing their full creative muscle. A caterer wants to make the bride and groom happy and impress the guests so much that they will want to use him or her for *their* family weddings and other special occasions. When you free a caterer to present unique choices, you get his or her best work. So keep that in mind, and work with your caterer to choose original dishes and ethnic options that will make for a one-of-a-kind menu for the big day.

Theme Menus

Never underestimate the power of a theme menu. You can make your cocktail party stand out by centering it around a theme, such as a Mexican fiesta or "Arabian Nights" fantasy. Your rehearsal dinner might set new standards when you break away from the usual catering and offer a Japanese menu complete with sushi, gyoza, and beef, chicken, and shrimp teriyaki. Talk to your caterer to let him or her know you're open to theme menu ideas, and ask about any unique ones he's created in the past. Perhaps, if she won an award from the International Special Events Society for her Tuscany-inspired menu, you can borrow heavily from that existing plan. That will make your menu award-winning as well.

Pleasing Guests' Palates

Of course, you could build a menu of exotic, spicy food, but would your guests eat it? There's a fine balance to be struck between choosing unique menu options and providing a meal your guests will enjoy. Don't go too far, providing dishes that no one can identify, much less want to try. Always use cards to identify "strange" dishes, and what's in them. Or instruct food-station servers to tell guests what the selections are.

Know your guests and what they're likely going to be willing to try. Mix up the exotic with the standards, to suit all of your guests' appetites. That includes kids, too! Be sure to provide a children's menu if there will be several little ones at any events—choices like mini-pizzas, chicken fingers, and pasta with meatballs always go over well with the kids.

And speaking of picky eaters, some of your guests may be vegetarian or vegan or on the Atkins diet. Always be sure to have a few meatless dishes in your menu, and ask your caterer for ideas on selections that will be acceptable for several types of popular diets.

"We knew that many of my relatives were on the Weight Watchers diet. My cousins had joined as a group, so we asked the caterer to come up with a few diet dishes and figure out the points for each, which we printed on cards by the dishes. They appreciated it." —Anne, bride

I'm Allergic to Scallops

Tell your caterer if you, the bride or groom, or any members of your guest list have food allergies; for example, if you know your spouse is allergic to shellfish, you may wish to build your menu without any. Your caterer, knowing that in a crowd of 100-plus someone is likely to have a food allergy to nuts and nut oils, fruits, certain kinds of dairy, and so on, will likely suggest that you create ingredient cards for each platter of food, telling guests what the dish is and listing the ingredients. Guests with allergies will appreciate the effort.

Budget Menu Choices

If you're planning a wedding on a budget, you probably know the reception is going to cost a bundle, but you can keep down the price of the food and beverages by talking with your caterer about making smarter choices for less money. You're not resigned to choosing a plain chicken dish and a plate of pasta either, so don't worry about that. One example of a popular budget choice is a surf and turf. No, not filet mignon and lobster tails, but rather a combination platter of three jumbo sautéed shrimp with five or so beef medallions, and a vegetable and starch. Caterers say this is the smartest choice for those on a budget. Surprisingly, it's less expensive than its top-dollar counterpart. Other choices: lobster meat in a small pile atop fettuccine alfredo, pasta stations with delicious sauces, and so on.

Presentation Is Key

With the right "plating" of your menu options, each dish can look like it belongs on the cover of a gourmet magazine, and gorgeous garnishes can make even lower-budget or simpler dishes look more elaborate (and expensive!). So talk to your caterer about his or her artistry with vegetable garnishes, swirls of sauces, sprinklings of spices, and the like. The new trend in garnishing is using foods and sauces to create monograms of the couple's initial(s), such as using a stencil and cocoa powder to leave a swirled *D* on each serving of crème brûlée.

The Cocktail Hour

Here are just a few examples of the delicious choices popping up on many wedding menus. Use these ideas as a starting point; perhaps they'll inspire you and your caterer to come up with additional creative ideas:

Hot and Cold Passed Hors d'Oeuvres

Nothing's more elegant than having your guests approached by tuxedoed waiters presenting silver platters filled with hors d'oeuvres. Guests love being served, and the delicious choices you can offer can be more expensive. Sounds odd, but it's a proven strategy for getting more out of your budget. According to the experts, you can save 20 percent on pricier menu choices by serving them as passed hors d'oeuvres, since guests eat fewer of them when they're coming around on trays as opposed to set out on buffet tables. Some ideas for hot and cold passed hors d'oeuvres are:

Shrimp with cocktail or tartar sauce
Lobster strips with lemon-butter dipping sauce
Bacon-wrapped scallops
Oyster shooters
Fried calamari
Satay sticks
Moroccan meatballs
Stuffed mushrooms
Stuffed phyllo pocket appetizers

Seafood Bar

Here is where wedding event menus have gotten *good*. In the past, you may have seen such standards on seafood bars as shrimp cocktail, clams casino, clams oreganata, king crab legs, crabcakes, bacon-wrapped scallops, and so on. But today's seafood bar is far more creative. Just check out the following mouth-watering options:

Soft-shell crab in a microbrew sauce

Oysters in a Gewurztraminer crème sauce with green grapes

Bermuda fish cakes

Salmon cakes

Lomi-lomi salmon

Asian spiced ahi salad

Coconut shrimp

Fried calamari with aioli sauce

Carp-roe spread

Crisp-fried oysters with red chili vinegar

Seafood spring roll crisps with citrus dipping sauces

Steamed mussels, hot or sweet

Stuffed shrimp with tasso ham and crab

Risotto with lobster meat

Vodka-and-citrus-cured salmon

Food Stations

* Pasta bar with several different, original types of pasta (e.g., curly shapes, bow ties, and even whole-wheat pasta for those on healthier diets who avoid white-flour carbs). Sauces might include a traditional or seafood marinara, pesto, or vodka sauce.

- Carving station, with an attendant wielding a very sharp knife to carve off the following for guests: spiral ham with a pineapple glaze, prime rib, suckling pig, Australian lamb, or smoked or fried turkey.

- Sushi station

- Quesadilla station

- Spring roll station (beef, pork, chicken, seafood, veggie, and so on)

- Mashed potato bar (A favorite with celebrities: plain mashed potatoes are doled out into martini glasses, and guests choose from a dozen add-ons like mushroom sauce, turkey gravy, sour cream and chives, and so on.)

- Crêpe station (seafood, meat, or cheese filling)

- Panini station (*very hot* at cocktail parties right now. A panini-maker is like a grill press that flattens and cooks a sandwich, such as a ham and provolone, turkey and cheese, or a Reuben so that it's thin and crisp. This option is highly recommended, especially for children and the guys who love their sandwiches).

- Shish-kebab station, where guests can build their own kebabs using hot, precooked cubes of beef, chicken, scallops, shrimp, and veggies.

- Mini-pizza bagel station with a roll-through toaster (guests choose their own toppings)

Buffet

Offer hot and cold dishes for optimum choice, separating the two on opposite sides of the room, or having several identical buffet tables on both sides of the room so that guests don't have to stand in line as long:

Cheese platters with unique cheeses, including warm brie encrusted with walnuts, horseradish Cheddar, jalapeño jack, and others as listed under the Wine and Cheese party menu. And offer a variety of crackers and grissini. Some other popular buffet choices include antipasto salad with roasted red peppers, caesar salad, tapas, dim sum, salmon mousse, blinis with caviar, fresh berry basket and fruit platter, chicken satay, finger sandwiches ("sloppy joe" style, cucumber, roast beef, mini-Reubens, and so on), prosciutto-and-mozzarella balls with roasted red peppers, swedish meatballs, stuffed artichokes, quesadillas, chilled seafood, grilled or fresh vegetables with yogurt-based dipping sauces, and don't neglect to offer a plentiful supply of garlic bread, warm rolls, grissini, and other breads with softened or whipped butter, garlic spread, herb spread, or tapenade.

Dinner

Hopefully, guests haven't stuffed themselves too much with your terrific cocktail-hour selections, and they'll have room for the dinner. Here are just a few of today's most popular dinner choices, so use them for inspiration . . .

First Courses

- Salad: mesclun, Caesar, mixed greens with a mustard vinaigrette or a creamier dressing (give guests a choice)
- Prosciutto or smoked salmon with a slice of cantaloupe and a handful of grapes (the new alternative to green salads as it mixes a protein with carbs)
- Soups: Comfort foods are back in vogue, so soup is making an appearance once again. Choose from the following favorites: lobster bisque, roasted corn chowder, New England clam chowder, Manhattan clam chowder, tomato and basil bisque, onion soup with Gruyère or Swiss cheese melted on top, gazpacho, wild mushroom bisque, potato-leek soup, and even borscht at some ethnic weddings.

Pasta Course

Choose from a variety of pasta shapes and styles, but avoid linguini or spaghetti—they can be awkward and messy to eat. Create a tasty sauce, either going with a traditional marinara or offering guests choices such as seafood sauce with a lobster-meat garnish, Alfredo sauce, vodka sauce, garlic-infused tomato sauce, pesto, and other selections. Or give guests the choice of stuffed pasta: traditional or lobster ravioli, manicotti, stuffed shells with spinach and cheese, and lasagne with meatballs.

(Note: Hosts on a budget often eliminate this course, believing that people can have pasta anytime.)

Intermezzos

To cleanse guests' palates, most formal and semiformal weddings offer a break from all that flavor in the form of sorbets: lemon, lime, orange, passionfruit, strawberry, or a mixture of several sorbets (in coordinating shades to the wedding colors, perhaps).

Entrées

Entrées might be impressive plates of surf and turf, or creative combination platters. Consider the following:

Filet mignon

Prime rib

Crab-stuffed salmon

Crab-stuffed flounder

Glazed salmon

Potato-crusted salmon

Sirloin steak

Australian lamb

Crown roast

Coconut chicken

Chicken piccata

Chicken Français

Chicken divan with almonds

Stuffed chicken breast

Turkish poached chicken with
    walnut sauce

Flank steak

Grilled shrimp

Shrimp parmigiana

Glazed turkey with stuffing

Vegetable empanadas

Rolled beef with artichoke
    stuffing

Sea bass

Venison

Paella

Side Dishes

Side dishes are not an afterthought! A great side can elevate the entrée to a higher level, while a humdrum side can negate the points you scored with a beautiful main course. So consider the following options:

Garlic mashed potatoes

Sun-dried tomato salad

Artichoke hearts

Artichoke half with yogurt sauce

Fresh, crisp string beans tied in a packet with a length of chives

Couscous and quinoa salad

Cranberry sauce with bits of apple

Wild rice mixed with chopped vegetables

Risotto with mushrooms

Mushrooms in a beef glaze

Wedding Cake

The wedding cake is the focal point of the room. Grand and elegant, beautiful and breathtaking, today's wedding cakes are by turns traditional (that frosted three-tier white cake) and trendy (square cakes frosted with colored icing). The design is the couple's choice. You've seen plenty of samples in those bridal magazines, so you know that cake bakers are true artisans with frostings, fondants, and sugar-paste flowers and fruits. The cake should match the style and formality of the wedding—a chocolate-frosted cake *can* work for a formal wedding—but the mark of a truly great wedding cake is its flavor.

We've come a long way from the standard wedding cake of yesteryear: the white cake with the strawberry filling. Traditional couples can still go this route, but they'll find that their peers are going for more individuality. I spoke with Ron Ben-Israel of Ron Ben-Israel Cakes in New York City, who told me that couples are choosing unique flavors inspired by their own favorite daily treats: cakes that borrow from Mounds Bars, for instance, with chocolate and coconut. Couples are even coming to cake bakers with requests for cakes that mimic their favorite Ben and Jerry's flavors, like Chunky Monkey.

Cake flavors themselves range from chocolate to lemon and carrot, and may include cannoli filling, fruit fillings, custards, and chocolate mousses with chocolate chips (a favorite). Texture is the order of the day; creamy fillings are given a little bit of crunch courtesy of added chocolate, white chocolate, peanut butter, butterscotch chips, or candies. Passionfruit fillings work well for outdoor beach weddings, and even ice cream fillings are on couples' order sheets.

Meet with several cake bakers, look at their offerings, and sit down for cake tastings with the professionals to decide the perfect flavors and appearance for the wedding cake.

As for topping the cake, it could be done by the artisan with sugar-paste flowers, elaborate piping of frostings (even matching the design of the bride's wedding-gown lace or as a monogram on the cake), or a cascade of fresh flowers tumbling down the layers of the cake. Those little bride-and-groom dolls are out; they have been replaced by other unique selections, such as flags of the couple's home countries, crystal figurines, and custom-crafted chocolate sculptures in a shape that matches the wedding's theme. Your cake artist can advise you and lead you to wonderful designs.

Additional Desserts

In addition to the wedding cake, you might wish to provide a groom's cake, a separate cake usually designed to reflect one of the groom's interests; for example, if the groom is a golf enthusiast, the cake can be designed to look like a golf bag. If he's a car-racing fan, the cake can be made into the shape of a race car and frosted in the colors and number of his favorite driver.

A traditional idea is the Viennese table, an elaborate spread of luscious desserts from tarts and cakes, mousses and pies, petits fours, pastries, and any other dessert you can imagine.

For an added bit of drama for the dessert hour, you might have the servers wheel out presentations of bananas flambé, lighting them in exciting bursts of flame that delight the guests.

Or, go the simple, elegant, classic route that so many couples are choosing for their weddings, and serve only sweet truffles and chocolate-covered strawberries in addition to the wedding cake.

At the Bar

If this is the area you're in charge of, you'll first find out where in the world the best bottles of wine are coming from: Argentina, New Zealand, Chile, and, of course, California vintages and other regional picks.

Further, you'll get all the information you need to know about pairing wines with foods, checking out charts and articles explaining the science of pairing food and wine. This knowledge is an invaluable resource, and I encourage you to make good use of it before you decide to serve any specific wine or bubbly at the wedding. Be sure to sample your top choices at a cocktail party well beforehand, and ask family and friends to help you rate favorites.

Mixed Drinks

The trend in mixed drinks served at weddings is to limit the bar menu to the classics. You could open up a full bar with every option if your budget is unlimited, but it's recommended that you create a specific, somewhat limited bar menu. Perennial favorites include:

Martinis (standard or flavored, like appletinis)

Mojitos

Gin and tonics

Jack and Cokes

Vodka-and-mixer drinks, such as vodka cranberries

Daiquiris

Margaritas

Caipirinhas

Mint Juleps

White Russians

Personalized coasters have taken the place of those printed napkins and matchbooks, with guests getting their own to take home. Choose from a variety of artistic graphic styles—and fun wording for less formal weddings—at the following sources: The MoMA store, 800-447-6662, www.momastore.org (my favorite for art prints and modern art graphics); Alphabets, 800-419-3989; Pearl River, 800-878-2446, www. pearlriver.com (for Asian-themed coasters); and a playful choice, chalkboard coasters, that have chalk, which guests can use to write their own messages (encourages mingling and gives kids something to do!), available at Uncommon Goods, 888-365-0056, www.uncommongoods.com.

Talk to your bar manager to create your limited menu of mixed drinks, and then print out a bar card to inform your guests of their choices. More creative couples like to name their drinks, such as Michael's Martini and Christine's Cosmopolitan.

You should also know that hosts are dressing up their champagne adding drop-ins like strawberries or pomegranate seeds, a blush or bright shade with a shot of strawberry or pomegranate juice, or peach nectar to coordinate champagne cocktails with the wedding décor.

Soft Drinks and Water

Always be sure your bar is well-stocked with plenty of soft drinks, seltzers, club soda, and bottled water for guests who don't want to get drunk. That water will come in handy at outdoor weddings when it is hot; ask your bartenders to serve it with slices of lemon, fruit, and other garnishes.

Coffees and After-Dinner Drinks

Espresso

Cappuccino

Flavored coffees

Irish coffee

Jamaican coffee

Chai

Bailey's Irish Cream, straight or
added to coffee

Cognac

Brandy

Anisette

Check www.foodtv.com for more suggestions and recipes for mixed after-dinner drinks!

Additional Wedding-Weekend Event Menus

The Breakfast, Brunch, or Luncheon

For this style of party, feel free to borrow from any of the aforementioned sections, as many choices are the same. In addition, you might offer:

Pecan or blueberry waffles or pancakes

Crème brûlée waffles

Blini filled with cheese or berries

Omelettes filled with choice of ham, cheese, peppers, onions, jalapeños, and so on

Carving station with ham or beef

Corned beef hash

Bacon, sausage, Taylor ham, Canadian ham

Hash browns or home-style potatoes

Afternoon Tea

For a high-style afternoon tea party, serve finger sandwiches, quiches, and elegant soups, along with a variety of teas and hot spiced ciders, coffee, and cool drinks.

Tea options might include fruit-based teas, green tea, mint tea, ginger tea, and good ol' Earl Grey.

Wine and Cheese Cocktail Party

Warmed brie

Brie en brioche (pastry-covered) with mushrooms or garlic in the cheese

Wine-infused cheeses

Creamy spread cheese mixed with caviar or spices

Garlic herb spread cheese

Herbed goat cheese dip

Spinach dip

Smoked salmon and cream cheese dip

Aged Cheddars, jacks, and a range of international hard cheeses

Pepperoni and sliced smoked sausages

Tapenade

Sautéed foie gras

Liver paté

Duck paté

Cheese fondue

Baked Cheddar-sesame crisps

Cheese-filled blintzes with berry sauce

Gorgonzola-stuffed mushrooms

A wide big range of fruits such as strawberries, blackberries, starfruit, cantaloupe, watermelon, and kiwi, all of which cleanse the palate and complement cheese flavors.

This sort of cocktail party should feature various wines and champagnes, cordials, and after-dinner drinks.

Beach Party Clambake

Lobsters or lobster tails

Crabs—cracked open and cleaned, served as halves

King crab legs

Steamed clams

Steamed oysters

Steamed shrimp

Clam chowder

Clam fritters

Hush puppies

Corn on the cob

Garlic bread

Frozen margaritas, daquiris, wines, and ice-cold quality beer

Casual Barbecue Cookout

Burgers and hot dogs, with a variety of toppings from American to Monterey Jack cheese, chili, sautéed onions, relish, and so on

Sweet and hot sausage

Pulled pork

Barbecued chicken

Barbecued vegetables, including eggplant, portabello mushrooms, and corn on the cob

Kebabs (meat or veggie)

Deviled eggs

Sides: garlic mashed potato, macaroni salad, tomato salad, fruit salad

Frozen margaritas and daquiris, iced tea, lemonade, wine, and beer

Asian-Inspired Menu

As just one ethnic-menu possibility, I've chosen today's most popular:

Sushis (including such delectable choices as grilled portabello and roasted pepper rolls, spicy tuna rolls with cucumber, Japanese pickle rolls, California rolls, Philadelphia rolls, and so on)

Tempuras (beef, chicken, pork, seafood, or veggie)

Asian spring rolls with peanut dipping sauce

Miso soup

Teriyakis (beef, chicken, seafood, pork, or veggie)

Garlic chicken with vegetables

General Tso's chicken

Gyoza

And so on . . .

Champagne and Desserts

Chocolate mousses, white and dark

Tiramisu

Chocolate-dipped berries and fruits

Chocolate-dipped cookies (Believe it or not, guests at formal weddings *love* chocolate-dipped Oreos!)

Crème brûlée

English trifle

Chocolate bombe cake with molten middle

Bananas Foster

Baked apples with cinnamon and nutmeg, topped with homemade vanilla
ice cream

Southern pecan pie with spice crust

Cheesecakes

Fruit tarts with chantilly cream

Assorted pastries: eclairs, cream puffs, rum cakes, and so on

Petits fours

Cupcakes with colorful icings and decorations

Brownie bar with gourmet brownies (Visit www.cherylandco.com for
terrific ideas!)

Apricot frangipani tart

Baklava

German almond and chocolate tortes with rum infusion

Truffles and filled chocolates (www.godiva.com)

CHAPTER 15

Putting On a Show

SO WILL A DEEJAY or a band entertain at the reception?

Some families love the traditional look, feel, and sound of live entertainers—a band in full tuxedos playing classics, standards, Motown, and Top 40 songs. They love the energy of live performances by singers and musicians who are *so* talented, you wonder why they're not international celebrities. From choreographed dance numbers to perfect harmonies, the guitarist's improvised riffs, and the lead singer's rapport with the crowd, you definitely feel, it has to be a band.

Others prefer deejays playing CDs or MP3s of the original artists' recordings; for instance, having heard Etta James sing "At Last" both live on stage and on CD, I don't want to hear anyone else's version of it.

A deejay's play list can range through every style of music, energizing the crowd and getting guests on the dance floor with songs that everyone knows from the first few notes.

Band versus deejay? It's all up to the couple.

But they may not have to choose! Today's entertainment companies have heard the dilemmas so many wedding couples have expressed in trying to decide between one or the other, and they've answered with a terrific solution: packages where you can have a deejay playing original recordings *and* have as his partner(s) one or several live singers or musicians for special performances. Problem solved.

Specialty Acts

A mix of a deejay and a soloist or musicians might be a specialty act to you, but you should know that weddings are borrowing heavily from corporate and celebrity special events—those amazing bashes you see on television—by bringing in entertainers of all varieties. Especially with theme weddings or weddings with a cultural flair, ethnic entertainers are the order of the day. Couples and their parents are seeking out the services of entertainment agencies to find out how to hire bagpipers, hula dancers, Irish tenors, and more. Here's a list of some of the more spectacular specialty acts that your team can consider for the wedding:

* Jazz soloists or trios
* Classical trios: harp, flute, and cello
* Individual classical instrumentalists
* Ethnic musicians
* Guitar trios or solo guitarists
* Pianists
* Violinists
* Doo-Wop or Motown groups
* A cappella singers
* Frank Sinatra impersonators . . . very, very hot
* Era-bands, such as a group that performs music from the eighties (Duran Duran, Cyndi Lauper, Madonna, U2 . . .)

Many bands offer several different kinds of shows in one. Their first set might have them in classic tuxedos or long black gowns for the women, playing dinner-hour music. After their short break, they come back in different costumes with a new sound, a new look, and perhaps even a new stage, such as a band that comes back in zoot suits to do a hopping set of swing music complete with the horn players doing splits and tossing their instruments to one another. After their next short break, they might come back as forties-era USO performers with the band in uniform and the female performers dressed up and singing like the Andrews Sisters. These blasts from the past and zips through time will please your entire crowd, young and old.

In weddings today, it's not just about having enjoyable music, something people can dance to. . . . it's about giving your guests a show, an experience.

Dance Performers

Giving your guests a show could mean hiring professionals to take to the dance floor and get the party started. You can search dance academies and entertainment agencies for the following possibilities (and more):

* Hula dancers
* Line dancers
* Salsa dancers
* Irish step dancers
* Ballet dancers

* Belly dancers
* Acrobats
* Eighties-era dance troupes
* Ethnic dancers

Music to Play

The choice of songs to be played at the wedding is up to the bride and groom. They should meet with the band or deejay to go over the professionals' playlists, request additional songs, and even say "No way!" to certain types of music they know they don't want played at their wedding.

When I asked several different deejays and bands what kinds of music were top picks among brides and grooms, they said the following were consistent hits at weddings:

* Eighties music
* Motown
* Country

* Classic crooners like Frank Sinatra, Tony Bennett, Harry Connick Jr., and Michael Bublé (This is the best wedding-appropriate music out there!)

When I asked about the popular music of today, the songs played on the radio, the deejays and band members shook their heads. It seems that while some current songs were on couples' playlists, overall the choice is usually retro, the best songs from the past.

Here is where you can record your most-wished-for songs to be played at the wedding:

* _____

* _____

* _____

* _____

* _____

* _____

* _____

* _____

* _____

* _____

* _____

Songs for Special Dances

In chapter 24, the top song choices for the traditional mother-son dance are listed ("What a Wonderful World" by Louis Armstrong is the most popular). While the choices of songs for special dances are up to the bride and groom—as is the choice of whether even to have special tribute dances in addition to their own first dance—I encourage you to check out the latest survey results on bridal Web sites to see which songs are ranking as most popular for the following dances:

- The Bride and Groom's First Dance
- The Bride and Her Father
- The Groom and His Mother

These are the standards, but couples with unique family situations are personalizing and thus modernizing this traditional dance schedule. Some brides might start off dancing with their fathers, and then their stepfathers might step in to finish the dance (or vice versa). Grooms might do the same with their mothers and stepmothers. Adopted parents and godparents might also be brought in for special dances. The bride also can dance with the groom's father, the groom with the bride's mother . . . grandparents . . . and so on.

The places to check for the latest information on popular reception songs are the biggest bridal Web sites where real-life brides and grooms e-mail in their song selections: www.weddingchannel.com, www.theknot.com, www.brides.com, www.modernbride.com, www.bridalguide.com, www.blissweddings.com, and so many other regional bridal Web sites, like www.njwedding.com. Research the latest song choices and ask entertainment professionals to provide lists of their own top picks, and then work with the bride and groom to plan the music that will help to rank your son's reception as one of the all-time best.

Personalized Song Choices

Some couples don't stop at just choosing their favorite songs from their favorite artists. Sometimes they bring in their own music. The groom might perform a song he wrote for the bride, or the bride might perform a song she wrote. It could be the sibling or parent of the bride and groom playing the guitar, or taking the microphone to sing along with the band's backup.

At one recent wedding, a karaoke-bar recording of the bridesmaids singing "It's Raining Men" during the bachelorette party was played for the guests.

Making your own music is not just an affirmation. It's pure entertainment.

Tribute Songs

Searching their own supplies of personalized music, brides and grooms have played at their weddings the following types of special songs:

- Their parents' wedding songs
- Their grandparents' favorite songs
- The first song the bride and groom ever slow-danced to
- The song the groom played for the bride after he proposed
- The song the bride sang to herself, which tipped off her friends that she was in love with your son

Music provides the soundtrack of our lives, and there are *many* more personalized choices than just those listed above.

Do It Yourself

For weddings on a budget, or less formal weddings where a band would be out of place, the bride and groom might burn their own CDs of their favorite songs—perhaps even making separate CDs for the separate stages of the wedding day (cocktail hour, dinner hour, dancing, wind-down). The CDs can be loaded into a 5-disc player and broadcast through strategically placed speakers, providing a great, personally chosen soundtrack.

CHAPTER 16

A Little Something to Take Home

OF COURSE, YOU'LL want to hand out favors to the guests, and the big sellers this year come in four different categories: delicious, living, useful, and giving. Sounds like a description of a good husband, but what's being described here are favors that will be *enjoyed*, not just placed on a shelf as dust-collectors. Couples and their wedding teams are putting a lot of thought into favors, now more than ever since many guests have to travel and go to some effort to attend the wedding. Giving a sweet little gift in addition to the experiences of the wedding can be a charming send-off and a much-appreciated token of gratitude.

Here are some popular ideas in the world of wedding favors. Take your pick, research your options and sources well, and think about personalizing them with labels, monograms, or little thank-you cards from the bride and groom. You can choose to go the do-it-yourself route with many of these options, assisted by a team of craftsy helpers for even more personalization and often a lower price.

Favor Ideas

Delectable Edibles

- Chocolates. From gold-standard Godiva boxes (www.godiva.com)—the hall-mark of wedding favors—to theme-shaped chocolates bought at a sweets store or confectioner, truffles or starfish-shaped raspberry-filled chocolate bites, the sweet stuff is the favor of choice among most brides and grooms.

- Frosted cookies. Wrapped individually or in boxes of several, frosted cookies are a hot choice. Check out the selection of flavors and iced cookies in pastel or sherbet flavors (coordinates well with wedding color schemes) at Cheryl&Co, my favorite source for iced cookies (and brownies as well!): www.cherylandco.com.

- Sugar-coated almonds in pastel colors. Sometimes called "confetti," and traditionally a good-luck charm, this choice remains a top pick.

- Candies. Willy Wonka would be proud of couples who are packaging up theme-colored packets of M&Ms, Hershey's Kisses, and Gummi Bears to hand out. This fun option returns to the sweet dreams of childhood, and is a low-cost treat.

- Chocolate bars. I had to set this one apart due to the wealth of specialty chocolate bar companies out there who will print up personalized wrappers for candy bars. Select from bridal, tropical, and themed designs, add the bride and groom's name and wedding date, and you'll end up with an ideal giveaway.

- Mints. From pastel colors to brights, you can find great mint choices at www.keepsakefavors.com.

- Honey. This is a hot wedding favor right now. Check out www. marshallshoney.com.

- Petits fours or slices of wedding cake and groom's cake

- Cheesecake samplers

- Cookie mixes (check out www.psaessentials.com)

- Add edibles to any non-edible favor: tie some candy canes to the wrapper holding a silver frame, attach a small packet of Hershey's Kisses to a gift certificate . . . it's a delicious accent and a little something extra tacked on to a traditional or keepsake favor.

Living Favors

* Potted flowering plants
* Single long-stemmed flowers in cellophane, tied with a color-coordinated ribbon
* A single gardenia in a Lucite box, with a touch of water to keep the flowers fresh
* A bunch of wildflowers
* Potted herbs, such as rosemary
* Flower seed packets
* Flower bulbs
* Tree seedlings
* Kitchen garden planters containing parsley, sage, and other herbs
* Vegetable garden starter: a basket containing seedlings of tomato plants, pepper plants, and the like
* Potted jalapeño plants
* Potted strawberry plants
* Bonsai plants
* And the biggest trend: potted bamboo shoots, large or small, straight or curly

Sweet-Smelling

* Candles and candleholders (www.illuminations.com)
* Sachets with potpourri
* Bath salts in pretty bottles or pouches
* Soaps (check out Crabtree and Evelyn, www.crabtree-evelyn.com)

Drinks

- Bottles of wine
- Bottles of after-dinner drinks
- Specialty drink mixes, such as Bloody Mary or margarita kits
- Martini glasses and bottles of flavored olives
- Hot chocolate mixes with packets of marshmallows
- Gourmet coffees

Frame Them

- Silver frames
- Artsy Lucite frames that have been decorated or hand-painted
- Talking picture frames (www.sharperimage.com)
- Frames with photo of the bride and groom
- Frame containing a printed poem or reading special to the couple
- Magnetic picture frames

In Print

- Books of poetry
- Coffee-table books
- Art books containing the works of the masters, or a theme such as seashore prints, florals, Tuscany, Monets, and so on
- Travel journals
- Daily journals
- Calendars with personalized graphics for each month, and all the family members' birthdays written into it

- Cookbooks from a theme region, such as Tuscany, Greece, or New Orleans, to share the culinary delights of the couple's favorite places

Moving Images and Sound

- DVDs or VHS tapes of the couple's favorite movie
- DVDs or VHS tapes that work with the theme of the wedding (such as *Blue Hawaii* for a beach-themed wedding)
- CD mixes of the couple's favorite songs, created especially for them with a personalized label and case
- CDs of the couple's favorite musical performers or instrumentals

Comfort Items

- Picnic blankets (perhaps monogrammed with the couple's names and wedding date *or* on a higher budget monogrammed for each guest)
- Top-quality luxurious robes and slippers
- For winter weddings, cashmere scarf and glove sets
- Fun-themed pajamas (One bride packaged these up with a gift certificate to a movie rental store, a packet of microwave popcorn, and several hot chocolate mixes and tea bags for a "cozy night in.")

For Theme Weddings

- Sunglasses for a beach wedding
- Snowglobes for a winter wedding
- A mask and beads for a Mardi Gras wedding
- A bottle of champagne for a New Year's wedding

Regional Favorites

- For New England–style weddings, put together a basket of pancake mix and fresh maple syrup, clover honey, and spiced cider mix

- For ski country weddings, make it a hot toddy basket with cider mix and a bottle of cognac or brandy, plus munchies that look like snowballs

- For New Orleans weddings, create a basket with fresh beignets, jambalaya mix, and a recipe for the Hurricane cocktail

- For Northwest weddings, smoked salmon and other regional delectables are right on target

- For international-style weddings, include hallmarks of your chosen country: biscotti from Italy, wooden wedding ducks from Korea, bottles of sake for a Japanese-style wedding, and so on

Favors That Give Back

You may have heard a lot about weddings where the couples chose to make a donation to charity in lieu of giving out wedding favors. It's a big-hearted choice, but there are some guests who feel they should get something other than a card that says, "We donated to the Save the Sea Otters Foundation in your name." Some of the more coarse guests might object to the couple's choice of charity—especially if it's in any way religious or political—not wanting someone else to make that call for them. I've heard guests complaining that they don't want to support ecological charities when they're in big business and routinely mow down rainforests to create their own profits. Others don't give a hoot about the sea otters. To that, I say, You can't please everybody! So stay away from the obvious powder-keg topics (like making donations to a particular political candidate) and choose the recipient of your benevolence with wisdom.

Check out any charitable association, to be sure that it's legitimate, that it gives an acceptable percentage of profits to the charity (and not to their own pockets!) and that the Better Business Bureau rates them well. Go to www.give.org, which lists the current BBB Wise Giving Alliance reports on charities that solicit nationally and provides regular updates on new charities. For background checks on local charities, check your local Better Business Bureau. For a written report, contact the BBB Wise Giving Alliance at give@cbbb.bbb.org.

If the bride and groom decide to make a donation instead of buying a standard favor, always attach an item to the printed card announcing just that. You can get creative with this, say, by attaching a stuffed panda or panda key chain to an announcement about giving to the World Wildlife Federation. A CD of whale songs set to classical music can accompany your announcement of a donation to Save the Whales. Some other worthy organizations include:

- American Cancer Society: www.cancer.org
- Cancer Care: www.cancercare.org
- SHARE, which fights breast and ovarian cancer: www.sharecancersupport. org
- Public Broadcasting Service (PBS, to support public television and the arts): www.pbs.org
- Nature Conservancy, which buys and protects land from urban sprawl, so that wildlife habitats—and our own adored parks and beaches—are not destroyed: www.tnc.org

---

What Goes Around . . .

Here's an idea whose time has come. The bride and groom can actually register for wedding gifts at a site called www.JustGive.org where users can list the causes and charitable associations they'd most like to support, and then gift-givers can log on just like a bridal registry to learn the charities you love and then donate in your name. Especially for the couple who already has everything and doesn't need any more china, Crockpots, or blenders, this site could provide a great alternative option to wedding gifts! For more on wedding gifts, see chapter 17.

- Habitat for Humanity International, which builds homes for needy families: www.habitat.org

Several Ecological Choices

- The National Arbor Day Foundation, www.arborday.org, will plant a tree in your guest's name, for one dollar at the time of this writing.
- Bookmarks and announcement papers embedded with flower seeds can be planted in a terra-cotta pot, recycled into flowers; check www.botanicalpaperworks.com.
- Tree and Floral Beginnings provides flowers, trees and bulbs to plant for living favors, www.plantamemory.com.
- Dried organic lavender flowers in chiffon bags with silk ribbon ties, www.organicweddings.com.
- Bamboo shoots are a sign of good luck, so find bamboo favors at www.romanticflowers.com.

That's a Wrap! Boxes, Bags, and Wrappers

Even the most modest favor can look extra-impressive when you pay attention to its presentation. A lovely, color-coordinated box, pouch, or envelope that holds the favor can give it added panache, especially when you add colored ribbon, bows, and an unusual label. Today's gift-box and gift-packaging industry is huge, and you'll find not only pretty printed gift boxes, but others shaped like pyramids, ovals, and a veritable potpourri of flower-fold boxes.

From silk-lined boxes to vellum envelopes, Chinese takeout boxes decorated with graphics, wax-sealed envelopes, voile pouches with drawstring tops, and velvet bags in rich tones, your options for packaging and presenting favors are unparalleled. An excellent site for favor packages is Bayley's Boxes (www.bayleysboxes.com), a standout among companies that make gift boxing an art.

Research packaging options at craft stores, stationery stores, art supply stores, and online, and find a style that's pleasing to the eye and also a great fit with the wedding's theme, color, and style.

CHAPTER 17

Gifts and Grand Gestures

THE WEDDING PROVIDES a chance to give the bride and groom a terrific gift. It could well be extravagant, such as the downpayment for their new home, paying off their school loans, or a brand-new car. Some parents go all out to start their kids off on the right foot in married life, appropriating some of the financial burden so the new couple can hit the ground running.

Other parents will give the gift of the bought-and-paid-for honeymoon, including special events like candlelight dinner cruises, scuba diving, and spa treatments at the resort where they are staying.

Here are some gifts given by parents to their bride-and-groom sons and daughters:

- Paying for an extension on the couple's home
- Paying moving expenses when the couple moves out West to start their new lives
- Paying for the redesign of a room in the couple's home to create a home office
- Big-ticket technology items, like a high-speed home computer, entertainment center, long-term digital cable subscription, or a home security system

- Cash to establish retirement funds, mutual funds, and other investments for their future financial security
- Supporting their careers by paying tuition for a specialty course or travel fare to a faraway conference

Gifts for Their Home and Lifestyle

While so many parents just go to the couple's bridal registry and buy the big ticket items that are left over on the list as the couple's wedding gift, others have taken the home and hearth concept a step further. Of course you want to help the bride and groom create their new home—that's what registries are for!—but you can do so in a whole new way. Consider the following real-life wedding gifts that other parents have purchased:

- Full sets of professional-quality kitchen cookware and appliances, gourmet knives, and top-of-the-line gadgets
- Furniture, such as the bedroom set or living room set the couple has been coveting
- Home office furniture, cabinets, storage units
- Landscaping for their new home
- Pools or Jacuzzis
- Back patio or terrace furniture (This one is a favorite option, since so many couples now consider their backyards an extension of their living and entertaining areas. Providing that Weber grill and great patio furniture, or an outdoor kitchen and a full bar is like giving them their own party area!)
- Wine collections, and even fully designed wine cellars complete with humidity and temperature controls
- Digital video cameras
- Gifts to support the couple's shared interests. After all, the couple that plays together stays together, so you can invest in the health of their

relationship by getting them memberships to a golf club or health club, professional-level golf club sets in His and Hers bags, mountain bikes, kayaks, and home gym equipment

Record your wedding gift ideas here:

* _____

* _____

* _____

* _____

* _____

. . . And Now I'm Giving It to You

We don't all have the budget to give the couple a full wedding *and* a Jacuzzi, so you might be looking for something with more meaning than monetary value. That's where sentimental gifts come in, something you hand down to the bride and groom that is very special to your family heritage:

* Heirloom jewelry, such as your own mother's ruby pin

* New, fine jewelry to start the tradition of handing down a family heirloom. It starts with you, goes to the bride, and then someday will go to your granddaughter.

* The groom might get his grandfather's pocketwatch, the one he used to play with when he was a boy.

* Framed family pictures, either recent family portraits or restored and framed pictures from grandparents' and great-grandparents' weddings.

* Holiday items, like the couple's own menorah or Christmas ornaments. Some parents have maintained a collection of ornaments for their kids, adding a new one each year. At the time of the wedding, your son might get all of his ornaments to hang on his own Christmas tree.

Grand Gestures to Make Their Day

And your big gift might not be a *thing* at all, a gift wrapped up with a bow, but rather it could be a special expression, such as a toast you'll make to the couple, a letter you'll write to the bride and groom that they will read once they lift off on their way to the honeymoon, a song you dedicate to them during the reception.

One family wrote in with their special grand gesture . . .

"We knew our son really wanted his college roommate to come to the wedding, be in the wedding party, and be a part of the day, but his friend couldn't get off of work. Our son was disappointed, of course, but he told his friend it was okay and that he understood. A few weeks later, we got a call from that friend, saying that he managed to switch work days by calling in a lot of favors, but he still didn't have the money to fly cross-country to make it to the wedding. We jumped right on that one, offering to pay his airfare and lodging, plus that for his wife and daughter. We secretly ordered an extra tux for him, and we made a secret change to the wedding program, including the friend's name as an usher. We had the friend and his family picked up from the airport and brought to the rehearsal, where he walked in and surprised our son! It was the greatest moment, and he told everyone that we had helped make it happen. Our son said that was the best wedding present he could ever hope for, and that we made his day that much more special."
—*The Diaz Family, Orlando, Florida*

If you can arrange for a surprise guest or two, that will certainly be a gift to remember. If stealth tux rentals or airline flights aren't in the cards, why not orchestrate a video surprise by asking guests who can't make it to send videotaped greetings. The bride and groom will love it. With Webcam technology, the wedding can be broadcast live for faraway friends and family.

Other Gifts to Get

The bride and groom's wedding gift might not be the only one on your shopping list. Plenty of people have helped out with the wedding, and you should definitely express your gratitude. Friends who have helped with the wedding as their gift to the couple should still get a bottle of wine or some other gift in return. Friends who baked, cooked, helped set up, or picked up relatives at the airport deserve a concete recognition for their time and effort.

And then there are Welcome to the Family gifts, tokens of joy from you to the new people who will join your family circle, including the bride's family and any new step-grandchildren (i.e., the bride's kids from a previous relationship).

Your own special people deserve thanks, too, including your parents, the groom's godparents, the couple who introduced the bride and groom, the wedding coordinator and assistants. Think about this; you may come up with others.

PART FOUR

You Look Beautiful

CHAPTER 18

Your Dress for the Day

YOU'RE IN LUCK! Dresses and gowns for the mothers of the groom and bride have gotten much more stylish and sophisticated than those dresses available for moms in decades past. That means you're not going to look like the First Lady from 1980 in a buttoned-up suit. Dress designers today are aware that the mothers of the groom and bride are not old ladies! You're as apt to be into high style and glamour, sophistication, and looking sexy as the bride is. You may be in terrific shape and want to show off your curves. You read the fashion magazines, and you know that women your age in Hollywood are turning heads on red carpets and at movie premieres . . . and you want to turn heads too. But before you start looking through bridal magazines, going to Bloomingdale's, or making appointments at fashion designers' showrooms, keep a few things in mind about the rules for your wedding-day wardrobe:

1. Don't attempt to outdress the bride. She should be the center of attention on her wedding day.

2. The bride gets a major say in what you will wear on the wedding day. This is purely to coordinate you more closely with the mother of the bride, so that you'll look complementary in the photos, match the formality and style of the wedding itself, and choose something in a color family the bride desires. And if she wants you in black to match the ultraformal look

of her bridesmaids in black, it's wise not to argue about black being bad luck. Keep it foremost that the bride's say matters most.

3. Speak up in a diplomatic way if you don't like the choice. While it's one thing to accept the bride's wishes for you to wear teal, it's another thing to be a doormat and accept a dress color that makes you look washed-out or frumpy. You have the right of refusal if you're unhappy with the choice. Simply go with a shade that's close to the one she wants, with her approval.

4. If you're getting nowhere with a bride who wants you to look like a frump, you have permission to override the request. Get a dress that works with the formality and theme, but choose a close color that works for you. Just tell the bride you did the best you could. Hopefully, she'll have moved on to bossing someone else around and won't give you a hard time.

5. Search for and order your dress early, so that you'll have time for any needed alterations.

Formality

You wouldn't show up at a beach party wearing a ball gown and a mink stole, would you? Well, the dress or gown you select needs to suit the formality of the wedding. Certain formality levels dictate hard-and-fast rules of dress. Here are the categories and their appropriate dress options:

Ultraformal (white-tie and black-tie weddings)

- Full-length ballgown
- Elbow-length gloves mandatory for ultraformal weddings

Formal

- Full-length gown
- Cocktail-length gown

Semiformal

- Cocktail-length gown
- Knee-length gown
- Dressy pantsuit

Informal

- Knee-length dress
- Pantsuit

Casual

- Knee-length dress
- Sundress

Of course, the time of day for the wedding will often dictate the formality level (see chapter 5 for information on times and formality codes), as will the location. A semiformal beach wedding could mean a dress, while a formal beach wedding could mean a gown. Always consult with the bride to see which level of dress formality she envisions for the day.

Color

There remains one strict rule for mothers of the bride and groom: Don't wear white. That's the bride's domain for the day, and while some brides might invite their mothers to wear cream-colored or deep ivory dresses to set them apart from the crowd, no bridelike dress colors should be considered.

As for the color of your gown for the day, again, that might be assigned by the bride, and she might even accompany you and her mother on a gown-shopping expedition. While most brides want the mothers to dress in similar shades, you'll want to discuss what that shade will be. During this conversation, you might learn that the mother of the bride has already laid down the law that you'll both be wearing pale pink gowns. That's because *she* wants the pale pink gown. But what if you have red hair and steadfastly avoid wearing pink? Or what if the color the mother of the bride chooses is just hideous, or if she wants you both in matching sequined jackets so that you look like a lounge act? As mentioned earlier, speak up. Agree to the style, but show them at the store that the pale pink makes your coloring look washed out while the deeper rose is a color you prefer. Dealing with this is a challenge many mothers—stunned by the battling egos and power struggles—have faced. Stay calm and press for the dress in a color that suits you.

Which colors are popular for which times of year? Pastels work well for spring and summer, with lilac, rose, and sky blue leading the pack. Deep hunter greens, navy blues, chocolates, and especially cranberries and burgundies are the colors of choice for fall weddings, with metallic shades of copper and silver topping most brides' lists. In winter, it can be burgundy and hunter green again, deep navy, red, and black (if the bride wants that formal look).

Add to the color of the dress a particular sheen in the fabric, and your choice of gown can glitter without sequins. Crystal and pearl beading delicately accent the bodice or skirt. Look at many designs, see which kinds of accents the dress affords, and let the choice jump off the page (or out of the racks) at you.

The bottom line: You know which colors look best on you. You've probably built your wardrobe around them. Stick with what you know, follow your instinct, but open your mind to colors you just have never considered wearing. You do get veto power, so be a good sport and try that orange chiffon dress before damning its designer. You might discover that you look great in a deep shade of burnt orange!

Dress Styles

As wonderful as the deep, rich, and bright colors of gowns are today, nothing beats the couture styles of dresses you have to choose from. This is the best-ever time to be a mother of the groom, since you have so many style choices. Here are just a few of the many options you'll find out there . . .

- Strapless
- Sleeveless
- Form-fitting
- A-line
- Halter-top
- Plunging backline

- Sexy necklines
- Old Hollywood glamour, like something Grace Kelly or Audrey Hepburn would wear
- Two-piece dresses with coordinating tops and skirts

The list goes on and on. And here are some descriptions of gowns mothers are wearing to their upcoming wedding events:

"A taffeta portrait-neckline blouse paired with a crêpe skirt. It's royal blue, and the skirt is cut daringly high. I feel very sexy in this outfit and can't wait for my husband to see me in it."

"A long black skirt, very form-fitting, with a white organza wrap blouse."

"A chiffon column dress in fire-engine red for my daughter's New Year's Eve wedding. The maids will be in red too!"

"A champagne-colored corset-type top with pearl beading, and a flowing champagne-colored ball-gown skirt with lots of swish when I move!"

"I'm traditional, so I wanted a suit dress with pearls. My future daughter-in-law took me to a designer where I found something exquisite in a cream color with a darker cream satin lapel. It was just like Diane Keaton's dress in Father of the Bride*!"*

Accessories

Pairing the perfect dress with the perfect accessories can make for . . . well, the perfect wedding-day look. Here are some accessorizing pointers:

Shoes

Be sure the shoes are stylish but comfortable! You'll be wearing them for many hours, after all. Lower heel heights are always wise for walking and dancing safety, in addition to the comfort factor, and experts say that choosing wider-width heels are smart if any part of the wedding will have you walking on lawns

For the Full-Figured Mom

These dresses might seem like something only Goldie Hawn could pull off. So where do you find flattering styles that work when you're not a size 4? Several fashion experts provided advice for full-figured moms:

- Go for becoming colors that will grab attention more than the dress shape. And always dress monochromatically, avoiding any kind of pattern or even lace that will break up the line of the dress.

- Pair a sheath or dress with a jacket that falls to just the right spot at your hips to elongate you. This spot is different on everyone, so talk with a stylist or seamstress to get the length just right.

- Go with the flow. A dress with movement will be eye-catching.

- Pair structure with flow, such as a well-fitted top with a flare to the A-line skirt or ball gown.

- Enhance your curves! Make like Queen Latifah in the movie *Chicago* with bold colors and accents.

- Choose an open neckline, not a high or closed one. A square or princess neckline is often most flattering to women who have chests to show off.

- Use sheers or illusion netting if you'd like to cover your upper arms or a portion of your neckline. This demure look, most recognizable as one of Vera Wang's signature styles, gives many women a boost of confidence—they're semi-covered but still look ethereal.

- Go for comfort. You'll just know the dress you feel best in when you try it on. If you're twirling in front of the mirror because you feel great in a certain style, that's the one for you.

- Wear a full-body slimmer or control-top hose underneath. The new style is a far cry from the girdle of the past that pinched and restricted. Today's styles breathe and move with you, providing a slimmer look without discomfort.
- Copy the styles of your favorite full-figured, stylish celebrities like Queen Latifah and supermodel Emme. Flipping through celebrity and fashion magazines could turn up just the perfect style for you.
- Use your best accessory: self-confidence. When you accept your shape for what it is and love the person inside of it, you can glow and "own the room." So dress yourself up in self-assurance and make your outfit secondary to your own inner radiance.

or cobblestone pathways, marble stairs, or other tricky surfaces. The shoe goddess in you can select from a number of styles, from simple to strappy and shiny with jewels. It all depends on the right look for your gown. Simple elegance often works best.

Stockings

Choose stockings for comfort and shine and perhaps to give your legs a nice tan color. Never go too dark or too patterned, and save the fishnets for your romantic nights at home with your partner. Sometimes too much is too much. Check out designer stocking lines like Donna Karan and Givenchy to indulge elegantly.

Undergarments

The right bra can make your dress look all the better! So try on some supportive, stylish selections, perhaps even with the help of a professional. (You'd be surprised how often women discover they've been buying the wrong size, or that a slight change in size makes them look even better in their clothes!) Choose body slimmers, slips, and underwear that are designed not to show panty lines.

Jewelry

Now is the time to break out the diamond earrings and pendant, if you have them. The wedding calls for your finest, so don't be shy about showing off a bit. Plenty of moms buy new necklace-and-earring sets in shades and stones to match their dresses, and their partners sometimes give them *gifts* of fine jewels to wear on the wedding day. Keep your jewelry look classic and elegant, and if you'll be wearing new jewels to the wedding, keep them as potential family heirlooms.

Hair Adornments

From jeweled hairpins to pearl pins worn in a French twist, floral pins specially designed, and precious-stone hair clips, your topmost accessory can bring out the beauty of your hairstyle. Talk to a floral designer about creating a hair clip made with attached fresh stephanotis or a large, dramatic flower—and check out fabulous fake floral hair accessories as well.

Jackets

Jackets seem to be a staple in many moms' wedding day wardrobe, either as a part of her full ensemble, or as a planned extra to slip into during the evening hours of an outdoor or boat wedding. Choose your design well, and also look at the stylish long coats that fasten with one button in front. Try on several different styles to see which works best with your dress, and choose a coordinating color.

Gloves

For an ultraformal wedding, you might find yourself sliding on lush elbow-length opera gloves. Check at bridal gown shops for the widest array of styles, and look at accents like fabric-covered buttons. You can order gloves dyed to match your gown perfectly.

Hats

Hats are back in style! Think about the stylish hats Grace Kelly wore, or the elegant hats in the movie *Four Weddings and a Funeral*. There's something very elegant about a woman wearing a hat, and the wedding (or wedding weekend) is the ideal time to bring out your best styles. Not all hats are made equal, though, so be sure the hat works with your face shape (round face = taller crown on the hat; square face = asymmetrical brim; heart-shaped face = smaller hat; oval face = all options). You can dress up a hat to work with your wedding outfit by tying a colored length of ribbon around the crown, adding fresh or silk flowers in a bunch at the back, even gluing daisy appliqués to the ribbon. Hats are great accessories for outdoor and beach weddings.

Shopping for Your Dress

Shopping for the gown you'll wear to the wedding can be one of the most exciting tasks on your to-do list. Though you don't want to seem selfish, why not celebrate the fact that this is a special occasion for you? Enjoy that palpable excitement when you're searching for the perfect dress! But shop wisely, and consider some of the newest and best sources for finding the dress of your dreams.

- Bridal gown salons. This is usually the first place a mother starts looking for her dress, poking through the racks while the bride is trying on wedding gowns. The options in these salons range from high style to "Haven't you changed your inventory since the eighties?"

- Department stores. So many mothers of brides and grooms have success at their favorite department stores' dress departments that this is one of the best places to find yours. Especially during the months prior to the winter holidays, you'll find formal dresses in colors ranging from champagne to deep cranberries, navy blues, and blacks. Designer dresses are often found here, sometimes at a discount.

- Outlets. Fashions can be found at 50-percent off or more at the many designer outlet stores around the country. So look for your nearest outlet-store mecca and start shopping!

- Little dress shops. Sometimes it's that cute little shop around the corner that has a small but ideal selection of formal dresses. Many mothers (and brides) have written in to tell me about their finds of a lifetime in little boutiques just around the corner from major bridal gown stores.

Alterations

One benefit of buying your dress in a bridal salon is that alterations often are free and done on-site by their team of seamstresses. This can be a great perk, as a beautiful gown needs to be fitted to your shape for its best appearance. A little nip and tuck here and there can make the dress look like it was custom-made for you.

If you buy off the rack at a department store or boutique, you might opt to take the dress to your own seamstress, or one at your dry cleaner, for the hem and any alterations that it needs. Consider this a great investment in the perfect hang and flow of your dress, to bring out its best movement.

Your Rehearsal-Dinner Outfit

As mentioned earlier, the wedding day isn't the only time to wear a gorgeous dress. You'll want to look beautiful at the rehearsal dinner too, so you should choose that outfit with your best appearance and comfort in mind. Some mothers buy a new dress for the occasion, especially if the dinner will be formal, and others simply spruce up a favorite dress they already own with nice jewelry. For less formal rehearsal dinners, any outfit you'd wear to work is fine, including dressy pantsuits and perhaps even an out-on-the-town-style dress you feel fabulous in.

Keep your dress-up wardrobe in mind for all of the wedding events, from showers to dinners with the bride's family, bridal brunches, and meetings with wedding professionals. Often, your work wardrobe will provide all the answers, but you might choose to invest in a basic black dress that will work for many different occasions.

Casual Attire for the Wedding Weekend

So what does "casual nice" mean? How about "smart casual"? For the many events of the wedding weekend, from tours around town to brunches and wine and cheese parties, "casual nice" is likely to be the dress code you give your guests. To you, it could mean a pair of nice black pants and a baby-blue cashmere sweater, or a pair of khaki pants and a crisp white button-down sleeveless shirt with a yellow sweater tied around your shoulders. What would you wear if you were meeting a friend for lunch at a trendy bistro? That question usually leads you to the perfect wedding-weekend outfit.

Sundresses are popular with moms attending outdoor luncheons or picnics, and a great pair of jeans with a fun T-shirt is ideal for the family softball tournament. Be casual, feel smart, and look nice.

CHAPTER 19

Beautiful Touches

ONCE AGAIN, IT'S NOT just about how beautiful your dress is, it's how beautiful you look . . . and feel!

It's time for you to look great. (Okay, so you're already beautiful—especially to your partner and kids) but the wedding calls for a little polish to your everyday perfection. And that applies not just to the wedding day itself, but to all of the events leading up to it: the engagement party, meeting the bride's parents, bridal brunches, the wedding-weekend events, the rehearsal and rehearsal dinner. You'll be glowing and radiant at every one of them!

In case you want to join the ranks of moms who (just like all those brides-to-be out there!) start working *now* on themselves to look more glamorous/younger/fresher/more "now"/thinner when the wedding weekend rolls around, this section will get you thinking about and scheduling your own beauty strategies.

Some moms jump on the weight-loss track, others start bleaching their teeth, others start getting facials, and others get their eyes "done." While you might not be among those who hightail it to the plastic surgeon's office (or, you might be!) here are some pointers on the path to looking and feeling your best.

Skin Care

Healthy, glowing skin is the foundation for your beauty. So take the time now to either step up or establish a great skin-care regimen. Start by consulting with a dermatologist or skin aesthetician who can assess your skin's needs and perhaps recommend or prescribe products that will bring out your best look. With the help of a skin-care professional, you'll find out just which creams for wrinkle-reducing, pore-refining, blemish-reducing, and undereye-circle eliminating are worth your time and expense.

It goes beyond your face, too. Your body—your arms, legs, torso, shoulders, neck, and so on—can be baby smooth with just a few weeks or months of TLC. So look into exfoliators, moisturizers, fade creams, and the help of a dermatologist to give you healthier skin. As for tanning, the masses are staying away from tanning beds and all-day beach sessions, going instead for self-tanner applications done by professionals or at spray-on self-tan centers.

Practicing a healthy skin-care routine is not just a short-term goal, but should be a way of life. So research your options, identify the strengths of your own skin that you'd like to emphasize, and start now to obtain better, baby-soft skin.

Nails

Obviously, a manicure and pedicure is standard for most women headed for a wedding, and you should know that you, too, can get a French manicure or a color-coordinating polish to make your look complete. Don't neglect your feet, as a great pedicure can make the most of your open-toed shoes and the finishing touch for head-to-toe beauty.

Beauty Secret for Extra Shine

Check out products that are labeled as giving skin extra shimmer, such as moisturizers and "light-reflecting" lotions. These products can make you sparkle.

Tweezing and Waxing

Beauty experts say the one thing that makes a woman's eyes stand out and her face look younger without plastic surgery is the shape of her eyebrows. With the expert treatment of a brow-shaper or waxing specialist, your eyebrows can take on a whole new lift and arch. Visit a brow specialist for a consultation and tweezing.

Waxing and laser hair-removal treatments can free you from the daily need to shave, and these longer-lasting treatments can be worth the money over time. Laser hair removal is not as painful as it sounds, and you can request an over-the-counter numbing cream that works like a charm. Visit your dermatologist's office or a recommended specialist for an appointment.

Teeth Bleaching

A dazzling smile gets even brighter with white teeth. You can either invest in a pricey treatment at your dentist's office, where the whitening is done by a bright light or laser technology in under an hour, or you could embark on a do-it-yourself plan with whitening toothpastes, bleaching kits, or highly effective whitening strips. After just a few weeks of regular applications, your teeth will grow gradually brighter, coffee and wine stains will fade, and you'll have the smile of a celebrity.

Makeup

Sure, you've been doing your makeup every day since you were in your teens, but big event makeup is different and thus is best guided by a makeup artist. The shades and applications we learned decades ago might not be right for our changing skin tones, and since we stick with what works, we might not even be aware of how great we can look with a little change in color and makeup application!

> *"I'm embarrassed to admit that I had never used an eyelash curler. It looked like a dangerous contraption to me. But when my makeup artist used it to curl my lashes, my eyes looked big and bright. I bought my own eyelash curler the next day."*
> —*Jeannine, mother of the bride*

Go with a Pro

I'd advise you to always make an appointment with a qualified makeup artist who's been trained and licensed in the art of makeup application. While you can always walk up to a cosmetic counter at a department store, you should know that the salesclerks behind the counter are not always registered makeup artists. And their goal is to get you to buy their makeup. So they're going to say you need seven new eyeshadow colors, and that the lipstick you've just tried looks great on you. No slight intended to the many talented women and men who work at makeup counters . . . I just advise you to consult with a professional who is not motivated by sales to give you an even prettier face.

"I've always worn neutral eyeshadow and lipstick. I'd tried color before and looked like something out of the eighties disco scene. But when my stylist used a shiny hunter green liner on my eyes, it looked great. She used some greens in my eyeshadow mix as well, and it was just a fabulous look." —Sarah, mother of the groom

We're never too old to learn, and we're never too set in our ways to make a few changes in our daily routines. What you'll discover when *you* sit down with a makeup artist is that certain colors and applications you never even considered before were right for you all along.

Makeup Tips for the Wedding Day

You might choose to have the makeup artist simply help you select your best colors and give you application tips for your wedding-day look, or you could have that makeup artist actually do your makeup that morning. The choice depends on your schedule, budget, and whether you *want* to do your own makeup that day. Some moms say they love getting the star treatment with a makeup artist coming to their home with an enormous styling kit; others like to have their makeup done at the salon where they'll be getting their hair done.

If you want to do your own face, keep the following makeup tips in mind so that you look lovely, natural, and gorgeous both in person and in the wedding pictures and video:

- Use a concealer that is well matched to your skin tone. Your makeup artist will be able to advise you on the right shade and amount to use on those undereye circles, blemishes, and other skin problems you want to downplay.

- Use a foundation that is just a tiny shade darker than your natural skin color, applying enough to give you even, smooth coverage. Too many moms make the mistake of choosing a darker foundation so that they look like they have a tan, glopping it on and looking very "spackled" in real life.

- Use a well-matched pressed powder to eliminate shine. (Avoid pressed powders with shine elements, since these give a pale, masklike look in photos taken with a flash.)

- Include your neck and chest areas when powdering.

- Line your eyes with eyeliner, in brown rather than black, or darker muted shades that bring out the color of your eyes.

- Do not use sparkly or frosted eyeshadow, as that can make you look odd in pictures and—makeup artists say—can often age women's faces. Go with matte colors, and use a bit of shine just along the lash line if you wish.

- Use waterproof mascara, in a darker shade that matches your eyeliner.

- When using blush, don't overdo. Use a shade that brings out your cheekbones, apply to the apples of your cheeks and blend upward. Or, have your makeup artist give you application tips for your face shape.

- Line your lips with a lipliner pencil, to keep lipstick colors from "bleeding" into your lipline. Your makeup artist can help you choose the right shade.

- Apply a well-chosen lipstick color, blot, then reapply.
- Use a small amount of gloss on your lower lip.

Your Hair

You might wish to do it yourself on the day of the wedding or have a professional stylist set, curl, and style your hair. Mothers are enjoying the same hairstyle options as brides going for dramatic updos and French twists, and tucking pearl pins or fresh flowers into their hair. You deserve a crowning glory as well, so make your appointment to have your hair cut a few weeks before the wedding, colored early enough for the tone to oxidize into a natural shine, highlighted if that's your choice, and styled on the wedding day.

The key to wedding-gorgeous hair is a natural look. Oversprayed helmet hair that doesn't move is out, and sleek chignons are the stylish alternative to your well-maintained mane. You can try a new style or cut, but experiment long before the wedding to see how you like the new style. And as for perms or color treatment, always go with a pro.

The In-Shape Mother of the Groom

Like virtually every bride out there, many mothers *also* want to get fit for the wedding day. And just like most brides, this is a time when you might want to lose a little bit of weight and tone those arms, so you'll look terrific in your gown.

If this describes you, then I advise you to start thinking about a realistic and healthy weight loss and fitness plan. I've seen way too many mothers and brides go to wild extremes of starvation and over-exercise, threatening their health and looking the very opposite of their best on the wedding day. So figure out what you can realistically accomplish in a healthy way by the date of the wedding, and make a smart plan.

Your first step will always be to get an assessment by a doctor or personal trainer. Many gyms have professionals on staff who will test you in every area from your blood pressure to your fat percentages to your initial weight-bearing ability. A doctor will screen you for heart problems and other complications that

will dictate the range and effort of your fitness program. It's wise to take these
assessments seriously.

Once you're given the green light, then it's up to you to choose a nutrition and
exercise plan. Obviously, you'll avoid fad or extreme diets, just embarking on a
healthier eating plan—incorporating more fruits and veggies into your diet, trading soda for water, and skipping those midnight snacks. You'll choose which fitness plan works best, too, whether it's a regimen of walking and weight exercises,
swimming, tennis, or signing up for cycling or yoga classes. There are copious
options and plans out there, and the choice is up to you, but here are a few sources
that might supplement your fitness plan:

* Receive helpful articles on fitness and nutrition, calorie counters, BMI
  indexes, even access to your own online personal trainer and nutritionist at
  www.shape.com.

* Fit to Be Tied Online (www.fittobetiedonline.com) is a popular online fitness
  and health program where brides, grooms, and their bridal parties and parents sign on to get in shape by the wedding day. The site's specialized content and community targets the wedding-planning team with great advice,
  ideas, and motivation for everyone out there in the same boat as you.

Impressed by Fit to Be Tied, I spoke with the site's owner and president, Liz
Wendling, to find out more. Here is our interview:

*Sharon Naylor: Why are so many mothers of the bride and groom coming to
your site to get in shape for the upcoming wedding?*

Liz Wendling: Of course, it's about getting in shape and losing weight. But it's also that they know all eyes will be on them as well, so they want to go down the aisle with *confidence*, just like the bride wants that same self-assured quality. It's the mother's big day too!

SN: *The nutrition advice you provide is solid. Is there any special challenge a mother faces that would really make her want to focus on her eating habits right now?*

LW: One of the things we focus on, besides making healthier food choices, is what to do when you're under stress. When life gets hectic, as it will while planning a wedding, the temptation is greater to eat less healthy foods. We advise on smarter choices, which come in handy especially during all those pre-wedding parties with their calorie-packed menus.

SN: *Your site offers personal coaching to help reach diet and fitness goals. I think we all could use the one-on-one support of an expert when we're taking on something as challenging as reforming our eating and fitness habits. How does your site handle coaching?*

LW: I am a coach on the site. I provide one-on-one support for advice or encouragement. Clients can call or e-mail me, and I'll get back to them personally within 24 hours.

SN: *Besides the obvious, what are the additional benefits for a mother of the groom who wishes to join your Fit to Be Tied community?*

LW: It's a way for her to bond with the bride, as well as the groom and bridal party. If everyone joins together on the same site as a team, they can support one another and have something very important in common to discuss and share. Sharing with the bride and groom the legacy that taking care of yourself is among the smartest ways to build a life together with strong shared interests also is important. Health is the best heirloom to pass on.

CHAPTER 20

Keep Stress at Bay

WEDDING PLANNING CAN STRESS out even the most pulled-together, calm, serene mom. Things do get intense, and we can only take so much . . . especially when we're already dealing with work stress, family stress, and regular everyday life stress. Add in the push-and-pull of team wedding planning, and you could find yourself with your shoulders up around your ears, a knot in your lower back, and your jaw aching from biting your tongue.

Wedding-planning stress hits everyone at some time or another, and it only intensifies as the wedding day approaches. So it's best for you to have a plan, to make a commitment to yourself that every day of this process, you'll find a way to release the tension, reduce your stress, and just chill out.

Think of your stress-relief routine as recharging your batteries. Chances are, you already have established stress-relief routines . . . this isn't the first time you've been stretched to your limits. If so, just step them up. Be loyal to them, and they'll pay off in multiples for you. If not, then add these "ahhh" moments to your life right now . . .

* **Start practicing relaxation methods.** Yoga, tai chi, and listening to relaxation tapes or relaxing music are excellent options.

* **Explore the world of meditation.** What you might not know is that there are many different kinds of meditation. As a writer, you couldn't pay me to sit down on a pillow and clear my mind. That's not going to happen, as I

have an active brain that likes to jump around like a sugar-fed four-year-old at the playground. But what *does* work for me is walking meditation, where I go for a walk and quiet my worries by being very mindful of my steps and my breathing and focusing outward to notice the various trees, flowers, the ducks on the pond, the formation of clouds. That meditation gives my thoughts an hour off, where I'm just observing. Works like a charm.

- **Get a massage.** Find a qualified massage professional at the American Massage Therapy Association, www.amtamassage.org and sign up for a half hour to an hour of relaxing bodywork, where tension is rubbed right out of your shoulders, neck, back, arms, and legs. The mind works better when the body is relaxed.

- **Step out of Wedding World.** Remember that you're many things in addition to being the mother of the groom, so don't wall yourself into a world where your every thought and reason for being is the planning of this wedding. Put the planning book down, and return temporarily to your normal life, your hobbies, your relationships, your favorite TV shows . . .

- **Socialize.** Go out with friends and family. Research shows that having expansive social circles is good for your mental health, while the opposite is a contributor to higher stress and depression. So embrace your social network, and—important!—be sure to keep company with positive, uplifting people, those who make you feel good and carefree. . . . not your friends who are constant complainers, energy drains, and worrywarts. Happy people are stress-relievers.

- **Laugh more.** Laughter produces happy hormones to lift your mood and keep you stronger emotionally. Find ways to laugh: watch funny movies, listen to your favorite morning drive-time radio show, read the comics, check out humor sites on the Internet, or go to a comedy club one of the nights you step out of Wedding World.

- **Get sleep.** Don't skimp on sleep, otherwise your batteries will drain. Get a good six to eight hours of sleep per night.

- **Exercise.** Stick with your fitness program or start a new one. Exercise raises endorphins and can give a big self-confidence boost to further fight stress.

- **Watch what you eat and drink.** Eat healthy, stay hydrated with plenty of water, take your vitamins, and feed your body and mind what they need to stay at peak performance.

- **Have sex.** More feel-good hormones, plus it's an investment in the health of *your* relationship. And beyond sex, make intimacy a bigger part of your life if it has waned in the past few months. Romantic dinners, showering together, holding hands, and having deep conversations reminds you and your partner of your value to each other.

- **Go outside.** Find a park, a hiking trail by a river, a mountain with a great view of the sunset, or a clearing where you can see the stars. Stand by the ocean, which is a great calmer, and get some fresh air, perspective, and a dose of natural calm.

- **Be organized.** From staying on top of your career workload to keeping your home clutter-free, knowing you're organized can relieve extra stress in your life. If only for these few busy months, consider delegating tasks at home or at work, or even hiring outside help to make your life a little easier.

- **Be flexible.** Know that nothing in life can be totally controlled, and you can't prevent surprises. The more relaxed and flexible you are about the inevitable shifts and changes life throws into your plans, the less likely you are to be leveled by stress. Those who are rigid, or who falsely believe that they are in complete control, are the ones who have a more difficult time dealing with stress when the wedding day approaches.

- **Nurture all of your relationships,** especially with your other kids. Make sure you're spending equal time with others who might feel crowded out of your life while you're so focused on the groom's life.

- **Keep the big picture in mind.** It's not the wedding, and the napkins and the flowers and the cake, that are important . . . it's creating a great start to the bride and groom's future life together. So even if small things go wrong—the tulip crop has been frozen over in the Netherlands, the caterer can't get cod—take it in stride—at the end of the day your son and his love are going to be married . . . with or without tulips and cod.

PART FIVE

The Wedding Weekend

CHAPTER 21

Wedding-Weekend Activities

WITH SO MANY GUESTS coming in from out of town, and with our busy lives jamming our schedules so much so that we don't have enough time to visit even with *nearby* friends and relatives, it's a wonderful idea to plan several activities throughout the wedding weekend so that everyone can spend quality time together.

> "I wish *we had planned wedding-weekend activities! The wedding day itself was so incredibly hectic that I barely had ten minutes to spend with my best friend from high school—who I hadn't seen for three years—before I was being pulled away to take pictures!"*
> —Lila, *mother of the groom*

Don't miss the chance to catch up with friends and family, see pictures of their grandchildren, *meet* their grandchildren, and hear all about your nephew's first year in medical school. The same goes for the bride and groom, who on the wedding day might have even less time to sit down with their close friends, colleagues, and relatives. Giving everyone just the one busy wedding day to spend together is not enough time.

In many weddings today, couples and their families are planning an arm's-length list of activities to fill two to four days before and after the wedding day with plenty of opportunities to dine, play together, laugh, and spend relaxed time together. The memories you create and share with loved ones can make this wedding something even more special for all of you.

Here is where you can help plan a number of activities for the wedding weekend. First, a couple of guidelines:

- Keep in mind that not every activity has to be mandatory for your guests. After all, they'll want some downtime too, as this might be their vacation, so handing them a strict itinerary might be a bit much. Give everyone the choice of whether or not to attend.

- Mix it up between formal, dress-up events like nice dinners out and more casual gatherings like a barbecue in your backyard.

- Include the kids! Especially if the wedding itself will be formal and thus "no kids invited," be sure to plan at least one full family event where the kids can run around, play together, and get to meet relatives.

- Print up an official list of all the wedding-weekend activities, including date, style, location, dress code (if needed), the host and her phone number for RSVPs, and a description of what the event will entail; for instance, if one of the planned activities will be a guided tour of your historic town, write down some of the noted attractions on that tour, such as "Millionaire's Row, a line of mansions that were once the summer getaway houses for wealthy New York City tycoons and their families in the early 1800s."

- Plan several events at the same time, and let guests choose which ones they want to attend. The bride and groom might plan a martini night out with their friends, and you can host a game night at your home.

- Wedding-weekend activities can be listed on the couple's wedding Web site or by using online invitation sites like www.evite.com.

- Don't get too booked up. You may want to host several gatherings, but remember that you're going to be busy that weekend, and the rehearsal dinner might be your "big party." Share the joy and let others host as well.

- Always get the couple's okay before you plan events. They will be busy, and they might be upset about having to miss an event they're looking forward to because they have other obligations. On the other hand, they might be grateful that you're providing their many guests with something fun to do while they're running around to last-minute wedding meetings.

Wedding-Weekend Activities List

Here are just a few of today's most popular events, broken down into categories, for consideration:

Meals

- Formal dinners out
- Casual or formal dinners made or catered and served at home
- Pizza parties
- Barbecues or picnics
- Cocktail or happy hour parties
- A trip to a restaurant just for dessert and coffee
- Breakfasts
- Brunches
- Luncheons
- Wine-and-cheese parties at home or at a winery

Sports

- Horseback riding
- Golf
- Tennis
- Family competitions, such as a His Side versus Her Side softball tournament, mini-golf tournament, bocce, horseshoes, disc golf (check with your park commission for courses)
- Hiking
- Mountain biking
- Boating
- Rock-wall climbing

For Guests with Kids

- Trips to see the latest family or animated film. (You pay for the tickets and popcorn.)
- Movie or game night at your house
- Community kids' events, like plays
- Trips to kid-friendly museums, activity centers, or arcades
- Bowling
- Mini-golf
- Laser tag
- Go-Kart racing
- Slumber parties

Seasonal Activities

- Trips to the beach
- Drive-in movies
- Trips to the boardwalk for rides, games, and cotton candy
- Farm visits during the fall for pumpkin picking, hay rides, corn mazes
- Sledding and tobogganing
- Snowman-building competition
- Tickets to a local ball game, complete with a tailgate party
- Holiday concerts and performances during the Christmas, Hanukkah, and Kwanzaa holidays

A Bit of Culture

- Museums
- Theater
- Concerts
- Historical tours
- Estate tours
- Visit to a bookstore to hear a celebrity author read from his or her book (check www. borders.com or www.bn.com to find out the appearance and booksigning schedules at stores near you).

For Singles

- Happy hours
- Dancing at a club
- Watching a game at a sports bar
- Watching a game at your house
- Game night at your house
- Tickets to singles' dance parties or happy hours
- Wine-and-cheese parties at home

Several parents and couples have mentioned that one much-appreciated activity is arranging for a shuttle bus to take out-of-town family members and friends to church or whatever religious institution they are affiliated with. If your guests are faith-oriented, they will surely appreciate your providing the means and/or location and times so that they can fulfill their religious obligations.

CHAPTER 22

The Rehearsal
and Rehearsal Dinner

REHEARSALS, OF COURSE, still retain their original function—to give you all a chance to perform a few walk-throughs of the wedding ceremony. The bridal party learns where they will stand, everyone practices the processional and recessional, and the bride and groom get last-minute instructions from the officiant. The wedding coordinator might be on hand to direct everyone, or you could wind up being the one who herds all the excited, chattering bridal-party members to the front of the church, gets everyone's attention, and starts the proceedings.

The officiant will explain every step, and by the end of this crucial event, everyone should know what will be happening and when. Musical performers might play their songs, those who will do readings at the ceremony will stand up and speak their written lines, and you'll even practice your part in the lighting of the unity candle.

The Rehearsal Dinner

It used to be that the rehearsal dinner was the mother of the groom's only domain. Blocked out of planning the wedding, for the most part, by the traditional duo of the bride and her mom, this party was *hers* to plan. Well, times have changed in this area, too, and since the mother of the groom can be as much a partner in planning the wedding as the bride's mother, this party might be a group effort as well.

Whatever the arrangements, here is where you'll learn the ins, outs, and new trends of throwing an unforgettable rehearsal dinner. Here is what a few moms had to say about the party that was theirs to plan. . . .

"I was thrilled that the bride and groom said that I could have the rehearsal dinner as my own to plan. They saw it as a good trade for listing the bride's parents first on the invitation, and I wasn't going to fight them on that. The rehearsal dinner is where I got to use all the ideas that we couldn't use for the wedding, and I loved being able to set it all up." —Georgette, mother of the groom

"This was like my own mini-wedding to plan, and after all those months of compromise and biting my tongue when I didn't like a plan everyone else wanted, finally this one event was all up to me." —Anna, mother of the groom

"We had a blast planning the rehearsal dinner together. We hate to admit it, but the bride was terribly bossy while we tried to plan the wedding with her, and this celebration was a joy to plan without her. Did we mention how much we hate admitting that? Together, we planned the menu, did the decorations ourselves, wrote up trivia questions as a party game, and got cigars for the men. We had more fun planning this party than we did planning the wedding, that's for sure!" —Trish, mother of the groom and Kenya, mother of the bride

Clearly there's a lot of excitement in planning the rehearsal dinner! You probably have some ideas of your own already, so let's get into the details. . . .

When to Have the Rehearsal Dinner

While most rehearsals and rehearsal dinners in the past have taken place the day (and night) before the wedding day, it's now becoming more common to hold both the rehearsal and dinner a few days prior to the big day. Perhaps it's a scheduling thing, where the house of worship is not available for a two-hour walk-through and so couples are forced to take the day before. Whatever the reason, be it a scheduling conflict for the bride and groom ("We needed to pick up guests at the airport that night!") or even a day of religious observance, you're free to plan the rehearsal and dinner one, two, or three nights—or even a week—before the wedding.

Who's Invited?

Those invited are the bridal party and their dates or spouses, siblings who are not in the bridal party and their dates or spouses, the officiant and his or her guest or spouse, anyone who's performing music or reading during the ceremony, and the child attendants and their parents. Take time to thank everyone for their participation, generosity, and travel.

More and more wedding teams are opening up the doors to share this party not just with the bridal party and the people who will perform at the wedding, but also with select guests of the parents' choice. Some groups go all out and invite *all* of their out-of-town guests, and others limit the "outsiders" to grandparents, godparents, and other honored relatives and friends. The guest list is up to you, depending on your location, budget, and how big a party you want. Overall, most couples tell me they liked having smaller, more intimate parties where they could really spend time with their closest friends and family. So keep that in mind, and be sure to plan a separate event for those out-of-town guests if they won't be invited to the rehearsal dinner.

Where?

Again, this is a personal choice. While you could certainly choose to host the rehearsal dinner in your home, bringing out the good china and adding the extender to your dining room table—or taking the party outdoors for a good old-fashioned barbecue—many rehearsal dinner hosts opt to have the party take place elsewhere. Here is a list of possible sites for today's rehearsal dinners:

- Private party rooms in restaurants
- One of the hotel's smaller ballrooms
- The hotel atrium or lounge
- Outdoor restaurant terraces
- Sushi or hibachi restaurants
- Pizza places for casual parties
- Private party rooms at jazz clubs or cigar bars
- Private party rooms at a sports bar

The key is to have the use of a private area, so that your party is contained, any speeches can be heard, and there are no outside distractions. While home can often be the answer, you should investigate the many options in private party rooms for the sake of ambiance and privacy.

A Question of Formality

Can it be a formal dinner? Yes, as long as it isn't more formal than the wedding. The dinner must never "outclass" the wedding, so if the wedding will be informal, so too should the rehearsal dinner be informal.

Of course, most couples and their parents prefer to have a *more* informal rehearsal dinner celebration. After all, everyone has to get dressed up in their best the next day; besides most guests today prefer a more casual gathering where everyone can be comfortable, ties can be loosened (if worn at all), and "casual nice" attire is the order of the day.

The choice is finally up to the couple, so be sure to ask them what style they prefer for this party.

Do We Need to Send Invitations?

Even if it's not going to be a formal gathering where invitations would be appropriate, it's still proper to send out official invitations to the rehearsal dinner. For formal rehearsal dinners, you can print out traditional invitations using black print on ecru card stock (much like the wedding invitation), conveying the tone and formality of the event. Less formal rehearsal dinner parties call for more relaxed invitations. In this case they can be store-bought, of the fill-in-the-blank variety, or you can make them on your home computer using nifty paper, graphics, and a fun, color font—perhaps even feature a picture of the couple.

Or, again, use www.evite.com or another online invitation service to tell guests the what, where, and when for the party. You can also choose to handwrite invitations on personal notecards or stationery for a warmer, personal touch. Always be sure to request RSVPs by a date sufficiently early to enable you to complete the plans. Send out invitations to the rehearsal dinner soon after you mail the wedding invitations so that your guests can make their travel plans with this event in mind as well.

Setting the Menu

Depending on where the dinner will take place, you can either select a set menu with the restaurant, giving your guests a choice of two entrées or access to a dinner buffet (always a popular choice), or you can hire a caterer for events in ballrooms, non-restaurant spaces, or at home.

> "We have always used our favorite pizzeria for our family parties. They have a great catering menu and make terrific stuffed shells, chicken marsala, Caesar salad, and antipasto—we didn't even think twice about having them cater our party. Plus, they deliver and set up the Sternos under the platter holders . . . we didn't have to lift a finger!" —Estelle and Lyle, parents of the groom

If catering is your choice, be sure to use a family favorite that offers terrific food, or take some time during the weeks before the wedding to taste food from other caterers. Any restaurant can provide takeout, or you can pizzeria-hop and check out the entrées at local eateries. Just be sure you've sampled the merchandise and order only your favorites.

That said, be sure to vary your menu, giving your guests choices for each course; for example, you can order a cheese-and-vegetable lasagne to give your vegetarian friends an option besides the flank steak or lemon chicken. If kids are invited, be sure to provide something they'll enjoy, like chicken fingers, mini-pizzas, and plain pasta with sauce.

Or perhaps cooking for thirty guests is no hassle for you, and you love the idea of making your own special recipes for your guests. Maybe other family members want to contribute their lasagne, lobster bisque, or always-requested cherry cheesecake. The make-it-yourself rehearsal dinner is a wonderful idea— provided you have the time and energy to whip up all that food!—as it adds a special, homey, from-the-heart touch that brides and grooms love.

"We were so excited that his mom and grandmother were volunteering to make their special dishes for the rehearsal dinner. We didn't want them to work too hard, but we know them—they wouldn't have it any other way! They'd be insulted if we said no. So we and all of our guests sat down to what we called Mom's Greatest Hits, all of her recipes that we love so much and that mean so much to my husband. We had fried chicken, apple fritters, collard greens, baked string bean casserole with the little fried onions on top . . . it was amazing. And after the party, she actually gave me all the recipes for those dishes! It was the best gift . . . you have no idea how much that meant to me." —Aimee, recent bride

While a potluck dinner isn't proper, you can accept the offers of grandmothers, aunts, and the mother of the bride when they ask if they can bring a salad, an appetizer, a main course, or a dessert. That way, everyone gets to contribute their most-loved dishes to the dinner. Or you can have the best of both worlds: Have the party catered, but then make your own desserts.

Speaking of dessert, you have a number of options. Some parties go with the sheet cake, some with chocolate mousse cakes, pies, pastries, or a combination of all of these. The dessert should be different than what will be served at the wedding. Some couples told me that their rehearsal-dinner desserts were the highlight of the party: chocolate-dipped strawberries, white chocolate mousse with raspberry sauce, apple pie à la mode with Ben and Jerry's Chunky Monkey on top. Whatever the meal, finish it off with something spectacular!

As for drinks, choose great wines and perhaps champagne, mixed drinks, soft drinks, and quality coffee or espresso. At one winter party, the host offered a variety of different hot chocolate mixes with a bowl of marshmallows and a cocoa powder sifter at the ready. Get as creative with drinks as you would with your menu. Use some of the ideas from chapter 14 to make presentation count, and even the most classic dishes and drinks will stand out.

Toasts and Tributes

Here is where the rehearsal dinner really shines. It's the words that are spoken on this evening before the wedding that give the bride and groom an unforgettable gift: They get not only your good wishes for the wedding and their marriage, but they also may get to hear you say how proud you are of them. In some families, it's occasions like these that elicit sentiments from parents and grandparents that will be remembered forever. Such expressions of love for the couple make the approaching wedding day all the more special; they know they're surrounded by people who love them (and will *tell* them so) and want the best for them.

If you choose to propose a toast during this event—and I hope you will—you can wish the couple well, welcome the bride and her family to your family, thank the couple for allowing you such a big part in planning their wedding, let the bride's family know what a great job they did raising their daughter, and let your son know how proud you are of the man he's become. And get it all on videotape, of course.

> "I preferred to give my speech at the rehearsal dinner, with the smaller crowd of people I know well. I'm not one for public speaking, and I was afraid I'd cry (which I did), so I was happy that I chose to say my toast at this party." —Juanita, mother of the groom

"I was invited to give a speech at the wedding, but I asked if I could do it at the rehearsal dinner instead. I've been to many weddings where the parents' toast was very long and emotional, and it almost seemed like they were trying to steal some of the bride and groom's spotlight. But that's just my own personal feeling. I had no problem speaking at the rehearsal dinner and found that I was less nervous doing so as well." —Marie, mother of the groom

Even though you're a hard act to follow and no one can see straight with those tears in their eyes, the groom's father and the bride's parents are also most welcome to say a few words. It's a love fest, a time of "kind words for kind hearts." After you've all expressed your best wishes, the bride and groom can then take the floor and thank you, their bridal party members, and each other for the very important roles you've all played in helping their dream to come true.

And Now for a Short Film Presentation . . .

The rehearsal dinner is such a relaxed gathering that it can be a time when friends and family share their favorite memories of the bride and groom, or they can talk about what they thought when the bride and groom first met. These personal anecdotes add life and depth, familiarity, and personalization to the party. And you can take this charming banter one step further by putting it on film. That's right . . . with the help of a friend who knows how to edit videotape footage onto a VHS, DVD, or CD-ROM using their own home equipment or that at the office, you can surprise the couple with a video presentation. Here's how:

Have a friend or relative (or yourself) interview the bride and groom's friends and family in advance of the party. Have them share their favorite stories about the couple and wish the couple well for the future. Some friends will ask you to videotape them in unique places; for example, a friend of the groom might want to be taped at the bar where they used to go for happy hour. The bridesmaids might have you tape them while they're all at the salon getting their manicures—a typical activity they do with the bride. One groomsman requested his interview to take place on the bleachers of the high school football field where he and the groom played ball when they were teenagers. He shared a special story about the groom that few people knew: The groom was the only guy in the locker room who didn't tell stories about his girlfriend (now the bride), showing his decency and respect for her even at that young age. The bride loved that segment!

Once the interviews are taped, grab some home-movie footage of the groom as a little boy, and ask the bride's parents for some of her as well. Add in still photos of each as children and teenagers, all set against a background of fun music, and you have the makings for a hit at the party. Keep it relatively short . . . no more than fifteen minutes, and watch those eyes start tearing. Listen to the sound of everyone laughing, and watch the bride and groom hug each other and point at the screen. Everyone is a star that night.

Gifts for All

The rehearsal dinner is traditionally where the bride and groom give out their gifts to the bridesmaids, attendants, and groomsmen; you may also find yourself on the receiving end of a "trinket" or two. (One couple gave their parents trips to Disneyworld as their thank-you gifts. For all their hard work planning the wedding, those parents deserved to say "We're going to Disneyworld!" when asked what they'd do after the wedding.)

This is also the perfect time and place for you to give your gift to the bride and groom. If you want to share your lavish gift with everyone—the balance of the downpayment for their new house or paying their honeymoon expenses, raise your glass and tell the world. If you're handing the bride your own mother's pearl pin as a family heirloom, welcoming her to the family, that, too, should be a shared moment.

You might choose not to share such lavish offerings with the whole room. To you, the time and place for gift-giving should be in private with just the bride and groom. If this is your preference, steal them away for a moment during the rehearsal dinner and give them their gift.

Favors

If you would like to give out favors to guests at the party—always a gracious and generous idea when you're hosting—check back to the favor ideas in chapter 16.

If the rehearsal dinner is the night before the wedding, be sure to spend some time alone with your son, talking over coffee or just chatting by the fireplace. If the bride and groom will be spending the night apart so as not to see each other before the ceremony, your son might be staying at your place. Make him feel welcome, and, if possible, make it a family night with all of his siblings in attendance. This last night in your household as a single man will be special to him and special to you as well.

CHAPTER 23

Before the Wedding

FROM THE NIGHT BEFORE to the morning of the wedding, everything comes lightning fast. You might think that after all these months of planning you have every detail covered and everything is ready to go. But not so fast! There are still last-minute tasks to attend to.

Use this checklist as a helpful guide in those last few hours before the big event, so that nothing is forgotten:

_____ Call to confirm all orders and arrangements with each of the wedding professionals who will play a part in the wedding day. (Ask the bride and groom which experts you should call, as they might choose to do the confirming themselves.)

_____ Pack a copy of your experts' phone numbers to bring on the wedding day.

_____ Check in with guests to make sure everyone has arrived.

_____ Check to see if guests need anything, like duplicate copies of directions to the wedding site. If it's something the concierge of the hotel can take care of, direct them to him. If you can send a volunteer to help them out (such as by delivering diapers for the baby, extra stockings, etc.) do so now.

_____ Review all contracts to be sure you're aware of balances that need to be paid on the wedding day, and be sure you have your credit cards or checkbook in your purse to bring to the wedding.

_____ Place any tips you will be giving in individual, labeled envelopes.

_____ Be sure you have plans in place for your own transportation on the wedding day (e.g., call the groomsman who offered to drive you and make sure he's still on board).

_____ Lay out your wedding-day outfit, shoes, and accessories.

_____ Encourage the father of the groom and your other children to lay out their wedding-day wardrobes.

_____ Make a trip to the store for any forgotten items regarding your wardrobe (e.g., stockings, a white shirt, and so on).

_____ Pack your purse with the essentials you'll need: car and house keys, extra cash, credit cards, and so on.

_____ Charge your cell phone and pack it in a bag that will go with you on the wedding day.

_____ Pack your own "emergency kit" including tissues, breath mints, safety pins, emery boards, clear nail polish, extra stockings, medications, your asthma inhaler or insulin shot supplies . . . anything you'll need during the wedding day.

_____ Confirm with the helpful neighbor who will take care of your dog while you're gone for the day.

_____ Arrange for a neighbor to take in your mail on the day of the wedding (robbers often target houses where they know occupants will be away for a special event), and also to have your outside lights and perhaps some inside lights in your home turned on during the evening hours.

_____ Transport everything the groom needs to the location where he will be staying.

_____ Be sure you have the bride and groom's wedding gift in the car, or make arrangements to have someone bring your gift to the reception site.

_____ Shop for or arrange any post-wedding party supplies if you'll be hosting the after-party.

_____ Do whatever pre- after-party setup you can ahead of time, if you're having it at your house.

_____ Shop for the day-after breakfast and do any prep work that you can ahead of time.

_____ Go for any pre-wedding beauty treatments, like a manicure and pedicure.

_____ Perform any setup or decorating at the ceremony and reception site the night before or early in the morning before the wedding preparations begin.

_____ Clean up your home to prepare for guests who visit on the wedding day.

_____ Be sure the lawn is mowed and the driveway cleared in case of visiting guests.

_____ Review any remaining tasks with your other children, the father of the groom, and additional helpers.

_____ Maintain your own stress-relief rituals (like taking a bubble bath the night before the wedding).

_____ Arrange showering and getting-ready schedules with others in your home.

_____ Leave plenty of time for your own beauty regimen, so that you are not rushed or forced to do your makeup in the reflection of a silver teapot because your husband is still in the shower.

_____ Be sure you take your purse, directions, and all supplies with you when you leave for the wedding.

_____ Go to the salon with the bride, bridesmaids, and other honored females on the morning of the wedding.

_____ Attend the bridal breakfast and picture-taking session at the bride's getting-ready location.

_____ Relax and have fun!

CHAPTER 24

During the Wedding

THE MOMENT YOU STEP out of the limo, many eyes will be on you. It's a fallacy that everyone's attention will be glued to the bride; your every family member and friend will be looking to see what *you're* wearing and how radiant *you* look as well. So even if you're an emotional wreck when you arrive at the ceremony site, be sure to smile! You only get one chance to make your grand entrance and your first, lovely impression.

One of the most charming moments I've ever experienced was at my cousin's wedding. As the bride walked down the aisle, her mother was escorting her. As they passed us, we all told the mother she looked gorgeous, and she said, fighting back tears, "I'm trying! I'm trying!" I tear up just thinking about how real that moment was, and how beautiful she and the bride looked together. They deserved that moment.

When it's your turn to walk down the aisle, whether by escort or as you're escorting your son to the altar, just be you! If tears are welling up as you smile, let them! A dab of your handkerchief is an honest moment. Sentiment and emotions are expected of you. It shows how much you love your son, and it shows the thoughts in your heart. These are tears of *joy*, and are nothing to hide with a too-wide forced smile as you bite the insides of your cheeks trying not to cry. Trust me, I've seen pictures of mothers doing just that, and they look like they're either sucking on a lemon or in excruciating pain. So let your true feelings show.

During the Ceremony

Enact your honored roles during the ceremony with pride and grace, lighting the unity candle, presenting the host, and/or performing religious or cultural rituals. You're bringing very important symbolism and meaning to the couple's ceremony. As you do, be in the moment. Notice everything about what you're doing. Make eye contact with, even wink at, the bride and groom.

Everyone is nervous when they play a role in a wedding, but the one big regret of mothers who let their nerves get the best of them is that they didn't remember lighting the unity candle!

> *"I was so nervous . . . afraid I'd trip, or knock the candle over, light my hair on fire . . . that after I went through the motions, I realized I really didn't remember much about lighting the candle. I know I did it; I saw the videotape. But I just was too nervous to pay attention and really enjoy it." —Sarah, mother of the groom*

Be Ready for the Unexpected

What to do if the best man leaves the wedding rings at the hotel? Offer yours as a replacement for the ceremony. Is there a misbehaving child sitting behind you, and the parent isn't doing anything about it? Turn around and politely ask the guest to mind the child or escort him outside. Misbehaving groomsmen goofing off during the ceremony? Give them the death stare as only a mother can do. As for all things unexpected . . . if you can't do anything about it, just laugh it off. That includes stumbling on the hem of your dress a little bit as you climb the stairs to light the candle. It happens to Hollywood actors going up to get their Oscars, and they handle it with grace. You can too.

This should be a moment you remember, so breathe consciously and notice everything from how the candle looks and smells to the cool metal of the host dish. And always look to connect with the bride and groom. Hold your husband's hand and notice his reactions too. That should not be missed.

If you will perform a reading during the ceremony, do so with a calm, clear voice, speaking slowly and remembering to breathe. Be sure you've practiced the reading beforehand, and use good public speaking skills to express your words, project to the crowd, and bring life to the reading on the paper.

After the Ceremony

Hug both the bride and the groom, plus the bride's family, and say something wonderful to each of them. You're all family now.

During the time for all of those photographs, as the photographer rounds up your troops and attempts to get the bridesmaids in one shot, the groomsmen ready to take their places, the bride and groom in individual pictures with everyone on their list, *you* can make the process run more smoothly by keeping the excited wedding party members on their toes, standing nearby, ready to jump into the frame. It's when groups are unorganized that the photographer has trouble keeping everyone focused; these picture-taking sessions wind up taking forty-five minutes and the cocktail hour is missed! As mother of the groom, you don't want that to happen! You put way too much time and effort into selecting that cocktail-hour menu, and you're all going to enjoy it! So here's where you can keep the picture flow moving, everyone at the ready, and the all-important portraits time to a minimum.

At the Cocktail Hour

Mingle, greet, enjoy! The celebration has just begun, and there are so many people who want to talk to you, compliment you, and congratulate you.

As you mingle with that glass of champagne or wine in hand, be sure to eat something! In all the excitement of the pre-reception party, where you're mingling and sipping and too excited to eat much of anything except a taste or nibble here and there at the start of the cocktail hour, it would be terrible if you were to fall into a common post-wedding problem for moms: drinking on a semi-empty stomach and getting tipsy way too early. Even if it's just a "buzz" or a headache from too much wine and not enough food, that's still going to affect the good time you should be having at the reception.

So be sure to temper your libations with regular trips to the buffet table.

Enjoy the festive atmosphere, pose for pictures with guests, and hug and greet your friends and relatives. Accept compliments gracefully and volley plenty back to the giver. If little things don't seem to be as you requested them during the cocktail hour, just take the manager aside subtly and ask for clarification. The bride doesn't want you running up to her all night to complain that the crabcakes are lukewarm on the buffet table, or that there are only three kinds of pasta at the serving station when you specifically asked for four. Unless it's an egregious mistake (the entire raw seafood bar you paid for is not there), brides and grooms don't want to be bothered. They just want to enjoy their party. You can bring any gaffes to the manager's attention on your own.

Remember, you're not working at this party—you're enjoying it. Accept that not every little thing is going to be perfect and that small things might be out of place. What matters most is that everyone is happy, enjoying the food, music, and one another's company. That's what makes for a successful celebration.

At the Reception

When you are introduced into the reception ballroom as the mother of the groom, enjoy your standing ovation and applause. You've earned it! Showstopping moms enter the room with a flourish, with some even asking their husbands or dates to give them a little twirl for added effect. How often can you say that an entire room applauds when you walk in?

And when the bride and groom make their appearance "for the very first time as husband and wife," it's your turn to lead the standing ovation for them, the couple of the hour.

At the start of the reception, the bride and groom will dance their first dance together, the bride might dance with her father, and you might dance in a special spotlight dance with your son. Keep in mind that some couples skip these spotlight dances with their parents, figuring they'll dance with their dads and moms often throughout the night. Some parents are shy about their dancing skills and would prefer not to be thrust into the center of the dance floor for a solo, and they're very happy about the couple's decision.

And then others are only too happy to get that spotlight dance. Some brides practice with their fathers before the big day, as do some grooms with their mothers. Couples themselves are now signing up for ballroom dancing lessons and having a dance instructor choreograph their every step, dip, and twirl. Yes, these couples want to make an impression on the dance floor and so, too, might you.

When talking with your son about your own spotlight dance, ask what kind of dance he prefers. The days of having only one choice—a slow dance to a ballad tearjerker like "Wind Beneath My Wings"—are gone and there is much more choice in dance styles. At many weddings, grooms and their moms are swing dancing, doing a cha-cha, or choosing to forego their one-on-one and leading the guests in a line dance they know well.

And speaking of preferences, you and the groom should discuss the song you'd like to dance to together. Is there a song that's special to you, a song that always reminds you of him? Does he have a favorite song that reminds him of you? The following are popular songs for mother/son dances:

- "What a Wonderful World," by Louis Armstrong
- "Moon Dance," by Van Morrison
- "Unforgettable," by Nat King Cole
- "True Colors," by Cyndi Lauper or the version by Phil Collins
- "Because You Loved Me," by Celine Dion
- "Hero," by Mariah Carey (especially terrific if you or your son has survived cancer or overcome another major challenge)
- "Just the Way You Are," by Billy Joel
- And, of course, "Wind Beneath My Wings," by Bette Midler

Flip through your CD collection to see if any of your favorite songs would be great for a first dance—fast or slow—with your son. And visit www. weddingchannel.com, www.theknot.com, www.brides.com, www.modernbride. com, and www.bridalguide.com to read lists and articles on the top choices of wedding music and special dance songs for weddings today.

Dance All Night

It's a shame when mothers are dressed in their finest and busily greeting the guests, but avoid the dance floor. They feel like they have to be proper and act with decorum, when, in fact, the opposite is what's called for! Moms can let loose and enjoy every song, and the brides and grooms hope they will. So while there's something to be said for being a good host and mingling with guests, it's also a sign of a successful reception if the bride and groom's parents are enjoying the music as well.

So switch into comfier shoes if you have to—the bride probably will too—and dance the night away with . . .

* Your husband or date
* The bride and groom
* The bride's father
* Your own father
* Your own special relatives, like a favorite uncle
* If you're single, ask that handsome single gentleman on the bride's side to dance with you (the odds of being rejected are low, since you're a guest of honor!).
* Your other children
* The bridesmaids
* Join the conga line!

Too many moms limit their own good time by waving away the bride's request to join the fun, claiming they're "too old" or "It's not for me." If you don't like the music the band is playing, request your own favorite songs. Crowds at weddings *love* oldies, Motown songs, eighties songs, even tunes from the nineteen-forties era. Just get the couple's permission first, and request some songs you know the crowd would enjoy.

Of course, it goes without saying that you should know your limits when it comes to alcohol. You certainly don't want to lose control and make a fool of yourself or the couple by getting just a bit too loose on the dance floor or even crashing into the cake table. Just remember to keep enjoying the food at the reception, and make the most of the evening. Have a blast! This reception is a celebration of love and family—and you're so blessed to have both!

> *"One of the highlights of the reception was seeing my mom and dad dancing a cha-cha. They dance so well together, and my dad really is a smoothie, so it was a treat for us that they really showed off on the dance floor." —Dean, recent groom*

CHAPTER 25

After the Wedding

THE HOUSE LIGHTS come up, the band says goodnight, the party is over. Or is it?

At today's weddings, the fun doesn't stop at 10 P.M. when your five hours at the reception site have come to a close. More on that in a second—first, before you leave the reception site, you may have a few last tasks:

* Complete payment with the reception site, the wedding coordinator, and other experts who collect their final balances at the close of the party. Sit down with the experts, the contract, and your method of payment to finalize your transactions.

* Tip those who will be tipped at the reception site—everyone from the waiters to the valets, coat check attendant, and cleanup crew.

* Be sure guests have a safe ride home. Call cabs if necessary.

* Be sure that *you* have a safe ride home.

* Check the location for any items forgotten by guests and take them with you for safekeeping and to return to their owners.

* Collect any throwaway cameras the guests have deposited by the exit in a basket, or left on their tables. Have the pictures developed and waiting for the couple when they get back from their honeymoon.

- With help, take the couple's wedding presents out to your car, and transport them to your home or to the couple's home.
- Thank the reception site manager and staff once again for a terrific evening.

The After-Party

The celebration continues, whether you and select guests go back to your house for coffee and after-dinner drinks, you join the parents of the bride and their guests at their house, or you join the larger group of wedding guests who are continuing the celebration at a nearby lounge or restaurant. Today the bride and groom often join these post-reception parties instead of heading to the honeymoon suite. After all, their alone time and the start of their "happily ever after" can wait a few more hours.

In some circles, the after-party is a big, pre-planned, catered affair, complete with a hired deejay playing slow jazz mood music and a hired caterer with specialty dishes. At one swanky, fully produced post-party, the bride and groom also chose to have burgers from Wendy's as their midnight feast, along with Twinkies and Yodels for dessert. Guests at that party said it was "so them"!

Some after-party guests change from their formal attire into more casual clothes, and then go out to bars, to a cigar bar, or even out for that in-demand fast food:

> "We took the limo through the drive-through lane at McDonald's! It was terrific!" —Lisa and Thomas, parents of the groom and Frieda and George, parents of the bride

Others climb aboard the bridal party's rented party bus for the ride back to town. The parents' limos might be long gone, so why not join the bridal party on board their rolling nightclub? Even the bride and groom might hop on board to get back to their hotel. It's an after-party on wheels!

Let the celebration last as long as *you* can last, perhaps into the early morning when all of you gather to watch the sunrise.

The Morning-After Brunch

It's so common now this is a must-have event. Parents of both the bride and groom can host their guests either separately or together at a breakfast or brunch the morning after the wedding. Most often, this scrumptious start to the day takes place at the guests' hotel (for ease of attendance) or at the home of the hosts. And again, the bride and groom often join the party before taking off for their honeymoon.

Black coffee and Bloody Mary's are welcome to those who enjoyed the reception and after-party a little *too* much, and those with appetites will feast on eggs Benedict, omelettes, blueberry waffles, crispy bacon, sausage, ham, bagels with cream cheese and lox, corned beef hash, home fries, blintzes with berry sauce, fresh squeezed orange juice, mimosas and—most appetizing of all—even more time to spend with friends and loved ones.

It's a delicious end to your wedding adventure!

Note from the Author

CONGRATULATIONS! You're now all set to help your groom and his bride create the wedding day of their dreams, and you've also started to create something even more important: the foundation of your future relationship with the couple. In every moment throughout the planning of the wedding, I hope you'll keep that goal in mind, always being there for your son (as you always have been) and opening your heart to everything his future path may bring.

I congratulate you on caring enough to be a part of this process for both of them, and I wish you luck and joy on this adventure. Thank you for allowing me to help you along the way, and I welcome any stories or questions you might wish to send me through my Web site www.sharonnaylor.net. I may use your story in upcoming editions of this book!

All the best to you,

Sharon Naylor

Appendix I

The Mother-in-Law Course

IT'S NOT JUST the wedding you're preparing for. It's also sharing your life with your new daughter-in-law and being a great and loving mother-in-law to her. Do it right, and your life will be enhanced; do it wrong, and you're setting the stage for monumental problems in the future. It's important to the groom that both of the most important women in his life not only get along but actually love each other (and him!), and it's equally important to the bride that she enjoys a healthy relationship with you.

If this is your first daughter-in-law, you might be concerned about how to approach welcoming her into the family and forming a relationship with her. Here to help you is a handy do's and don'ts list from Dr. Tina Tessina, Ph.D., a family therapist and author of *How to Be a Couple and Still be Free* and *It Ends with You: Grow Up and Out of Dysfunction* (www.tinatessina.com):

Do's and Don'ts for Getting Along with Your Daughter-in-Law:

DO be warm and welcoming to your son's new bride. She's as nervous about getting along with you as you may be about her.

DON'T be intrusive. Offer an invitation, then wait for her to offer the next one.

DO offer your help, advice, recipes, and so on.

DON'T insist your new daughter-in-law do it your way.

DO try to learn about your new daughter-in-law's tastes, likes, and dislikes.

DON'T criticize if you dislike her taste—what she wears, how she decorates, and so on.

DO tell your son what you like about his choice of a wife.

DON'T tell him what you don't like; instead ask him to explain the things you don't understand.

DO invite your daughter-in-law to get together with you and your daughter, if you have one.

DON'T gossip with other family members about your son's new bride.

DO allow some time for the two of you to get to know each other. If you live at a distance, write or e-mail to both your son and his wife.

DON'T panic if you don't get along right away.

DO try to understand your son's relationship with his wife, but don't assume you know how they feel.

DON'T expect theirs to be like your own relationship with your husband.

Welcoming the Bride into the Family

It's the little things that count right from the start when your son is about to be married and you're about to gain a daughter-in-law. *You* have the power to welcome the bride into your family in a way that makes her feel loved, accepted, and valued . . . something incredibly important to both the bride and groom. As I'm sure you can imagine, she might be a bit nervous about becoming a part of your family. She might be worried about how to strike up a friendly relationship with *you*. You can put everyone at ease with a few symbolic and sentimental actions right now that will pave the way for future harmony. (And remember, this will be the mother of your grandchildren. That's just one reason to embrace her now.)

Here are a few ways that you can welcome the bride into your family officially . . .

* Write a heartfelt letter telling her how thrilled you are that your son has chosen such a wonderful woman to marry and telling her how much you're looking forward to all the wonderful things to come now that she has become a part of your lives.

* Give her a special little present, such as a mug with her name on it to match the set your entire family has, or a Christmas stocking or ornament with her name on it to match your family's collection—something symbolic to make her "part of your group" and part of your family's rituals.

* Let her know it's okay to call you "Mom."

* Give her a datebook with all the family members' birthdays recorded.

* Give her copies of your favorite family recipes, including the groom's favorite dishes, and volunteer to coach her in the kitchen when she makes them for the first time (should she want help).

* Let her contribute to family holiday rituals, like cooking for Thanksgiving.

* Give her a family heirloom, like the groom's grandmother's silver bracelet, to be worn on the wedding day and afterward.

* Take special interest in her work, her career accomplishments, anything big she has going on in her life. Tell her you're proud of her.

* Tell the groom how much you love his choice. It will get back to her.

Understanding Your Son

"What your son may be thinking and what may change in your relationship with him, of course, depends on the relationship you have with him up until he prepared to walk down the aisle. Some aspects of your relationship may not change at all, but others will see a dramatic shift," points out Dr. Susan Newman, Ph.D., a social psychologist and author of *Nobody's Baby Now: Reinventing Your Adult Relationship with Your Mother and Father* (www.susannewmanphd.com). Dr. Newman has provided the following guidelines for understanding and working successfully with the changes your son is going through, with the ultimate goal of setting the foundation for a wonderful relationship between the two of you into the future:

What's My Son Thinking and Feeling?

To help you prepare and not be caught off guard, here are insights into thoughts (and fears) that could very well be occupying your son:

- He's likely to be worried about how well—or if—you and his wife will get along for the long run. Consider being the person who makes the first effort.

- He wants both of you (the two most important women in his life) to be happy, so on occasion he's going to feel pulled in two directions. Consider being the one to lighten up on the demands.

- He might be asking himself if his bride measures up to your family's standards. Is she smart enough, pretty enough, energetic enough? Is she as accomplished as you or one of his sisters in certain areas? Be generous with your praise and encouraging that your daughter-in-law will master what he may perceive as a deficit.

- He could be having generalized doubts about the plunge he's taking. Shore him up by underscoring qualities you like in his bride.

- In all probability, marriage is the biggest independent decision of his life and he knows it. Boost his confidence by reassuring him he made the right choice.

- He may envision a bigger happy family. That means getting along with his new extended family as well as with the bride, being compatible with his new in-laws, new sisters- and brothers-in-law, as well as assorted branches that may be in his bride's family. Avoid being competitive in any way with his new family.

- Difficult as it is to believe as you watch him step into another life phase that is more independent of you than any that preceded it, he may be afraid of losing you. Assure him you will always be there for him.

What Will Change?

Anticipate changes in your relationship with your son. They will, however, vary significantly depending on your prior closeness and amount of contact as well as on the distance you will be living from each other. The following are some potential changes:

- If he confided in you before the wedding, don't expect the closeness to continue in the same way.

- You will probably hear from him less, and he'll ask for your opinion less frequently. Be cautious when commenting or offering advice so you don't inadvertently demean or offend his new bride or her family.

- You will probably see less of him. He's now dividing his free time among many more people (in-laws, his bride's other relatives). You'll have to be willing to share your son and understand the demands on his available time. Compromise when you can to make life easier for him.

- He may stop noticing your new hairstyle (if he ever did). Or, if he commented on how you looked, or what you did, that may cease as well. His attentions are on his new bride—correct protocol for new husbands.

- If he's married a woman of a different faith or culture, be accepting of his choice and know that you may be asked to be part of rituals and traditions that are foreign to you. Embrace them rather than balking. Ask questions and be accepting to ease your son's transition. It's a change for him, too.

- Seemingly out of the blue, he's likely to act more responsibly. He may remember small things like your anniversary or birthday or to call his sister—all previously ignored or forgotten. Marriage adds maturity, but you may want to credit his new bride as well.

- For the first time in his life, he's helping—at his house or yours—doing chores and mastering tasks you could never get him to do. Silently pat yourself on the back; he was paying attention when you showed him how to hammer a nail, do the laundry, wash the dishes. . . . You did a good job of readying him for marriage and independence.

- When, on occasion, he reverts back to the little boy you once tucked in each night, revel in that brief glimpse of the past.

Appendix 2

Sentiments for Your Son

IT'S A WISE, warm, and wonderful move for you to express your joy to your son at this threshold in his life. Use this space to pen your own message of appreciation to him. You can then use these notes in a card you give him on the wedding day, or in a toast you make to him either at the rehearsal dinner or at the wedding reception:

Appendix 3

Wedding-Planning Timetable

One Year Before the Wedding

_____ Announce engagement.

_____ Attend engagement parties.

_____ Discuss with the couple and other planners what their shared wishes are for the wedding of their dreams.

_____ Meet with any family members who will participate in planning (or paying for) the wedding.

_____ Begin looking through magazines and books for wedding-day ideas.

_____ Hire a wedding coordinator (if you so choose).

_____ Choose the wedding date (and backup dates for booking purposes).

_____ Inform your family and friends of the wedding date.

_____ Figure out the wedding budget.

_____ Decide who will pay for what.

_____ Decide what part of your budget will get the most money (e.g., gown, caterer, flowers, cake, entertainment, and so on).

_____ Begin online and phone research for dates, prices, and options.

_____ Request brochures for wedding research.

_____ Create organization system for all wedding plans (file folders, computer program, and so on).

_____ Bride and groom decide on a level of formality.

_____ Bride and groom make up their own personal guest list.

_____ Bride and groom request guest lists from parents, fiancé's parents, and siblings.

_____ Create final guest list.

_____ Select and book ceremony location.

_____ Select and book ceremony officiant.

_____ Bride and groom discuss ceremony plans with officiant.

_____ Select and book reception site.

_____ Research and book rental item agency, if necessary.

_____ Create rental item needs list.

_____ Visit with rental agency planner to look at their supplies, choose linen colors, china patterns, and so on.

_____ Bride and groom select the members of their bridal party and inform them of their roles.

_____ Bride tries on and orders wedding gown and veil.

_____ Collect bridesmaids' size cards and ordering information.

_____ Choose and order bridesmaids' gowns.

_____ Choose a florist and meet with the floral consultant.

_____ Choose and book a caterer.

_____ Choose and book a cake baker.

_____ Choose and book a photographer.

_____ Choose and book a videographer.

_____ Choose and book reception entertainment, deejay or band.

_____ Choose and book a limousine or classic-car company.

_____ Start looking at invitation samples, and select desired designs and wording.

_____ Place engagement photo and announcement in local newspapers.

_____ For all planners, including bride and groom: Notify your boss about the upcoming wedding and arrange for time off for the wedding week or weeks.

Nine Months Before the Wedding

_____ Find out local marriage license requirements.

_____ Bride and groom meet with officiant about ceremony elements and pre-wedding classes.

_____ Meet with caterer to discuss menu, wedding setup, requirements, and so on.

_____ Plan beverage requirements and bar setup.

_____ Select packages with photographer and videographer.

_____ Select packages with entertainment.

_____ Meet with florist to design bouquets and floral décor.

_____ Meet with travel agent to plan travel arrangements and couple's honeymoon (if applicable).

_____ Apply for passports and travel visas, if you will be attending an international destination wedding. (Remind bride and groom to do the same.)

_____ Notify out-of-town guests of the wedding date so that they may make travel plans.

_____ Order invitations.

_____ Order wedding programs.

_____ Order additional printed items.

_____ Couple orders wedding rings.

_____ Have wedding rings engraved (if applicable).

_____ Reserve all rental equipment (tents, chairs, tables, linens, and so on).

_____ Choose and reserve a block of rooms for your guests at a nearby hotel.

_____ Book the couple's honeymoon suite for the wedding night.

Six Months Before the Wedding

_____ Order pre-printed napkins, matchbooks, and other items.

_____ Create maps to ceremony and reception locations to enclose with the invitations.

_____ Start planning the rehearsal dinner.

    _____ Research and look at party rooms.

    _____ Create guest list.

    _____ Create menu.

    _____ Create décor shopping order.

    _____ Hire experts.

    _____ Recruit volunteers.

    _____ Book site and finalize menu.

    _____ Send invitations to guests.

_____ Begin writing vows.

_____ Select ceremony music.

_____ Select ceremony readings.

_____ Audition ceremony music performers.

_____ Book musical performers for ceremony.

_____ Bride and groom register for wedding gifts.

_____ Bride and groom send for name-change information, if necessary.

_____ Book hotel rooms for guests.

_____ Book wedding-night accommodations for bride and groom.

_____ Arrange for transportation for guests.

_____ Plan "wedding weekend" activities, such as brunches, sporting events, barbecues, children's events.

_____ Begin pre-wedding beauty treatments: skin care, relaxation, massage, tanning, and so on.

_____ If holding an at-home wedding, hire a landscaper to do lawn, remove weeds, trim shrubs, add extra plants or flower beds, mulch, and so on.

_____ Make additional home-improvement changes, such as painting rooms, installing carpet, and so on.

Three Months Before the Wedding

_____ Bride and groom go for marriage license, according to state requirements.

_____ Bride and groom go for blood tests, according to state time requirements.

_____ Bride and groom attend premarital classes, as required by the chosen faith.

_____ If summer, holiday, or destination wedding, address invitations to guests now.

_____ Assemble invitation packages.

_____ Buy "Love" stamps at the post office.

_____ Choose and rent men's wedding wardrobe.

_____ Begin gown fittings.

_____ Choose shoes and accessories for wedding day.

_____ Bride's fittings begin.

_____ Bridesmaids' fittings begin.

_____ Help bride's and groom's parents choose their wedding-day attire.

_____ Choose children's wedding-day attire.

_____ Consult with wedding coordinator for updates and confirmations.

_____ Consult with caterer or banquet hall manager for updates.

_____ Bride and groom complete writing their vows (ideally).

_____ Bride and groom ask honored relatives and friends to perform readings at the ceremony.

_____ If you will be performing a reading, start learning it now.

_____ Bride and groom finalize selections of ceremony readings and music.

_____ Submit song "wish list" to deejay or band.

_____ Submit picture "wish list" to photographer.

_____ Submit video "wish list" to videographer.

_____ Arrange for a baby-sitter to watch guests' kids on the wedding day. (Arrange for several baby-sitters if there will be a lot of children.)

_____ Finalize and confirm plans for rehearsal dinner.

Two Months Before the Wedding

_____ Bride continues fittings of wedding gown.

_____ Bride purchases her "going away" outfit and honeymoon clothes.

_____ Address invitations to guests (for non-holiday, summer, or destination weddings).

_____ Assemble invitation packages.

_____ Buy "Love" stamps at the post office.

_____ Mail invitations to guests six to eight weeks prior to the wedding.

_____ Order or make wedding programs.

_____ Order or make wedding favors.

_____ Meet with ceremony musician about song list.

_____ Have attendants' shoes dyed in one dye lot.

_____ Bride and groom formally ask friends to participate in wedding, such as attending the guest book, transporting wedding gifts from reception to home, and so on.

_____ Bride and groom send for all name-change documents, such as passport, credit cards, driver's license, and so on.

_____ Meet with bride's parents for get-together (before things really get going).

One Month Before the Wedding

_____ Bride and groom get marriage license.

_____ Bride and groom meet with officiant to get the final information on ceremony elements, location rules, and so on.

_____ Invite officiant to rehearsal dinner.

_____ Plan the rehearsal.

_____ Invite bridal party and involved guests to the rehearsal and rehearsal dinner.

_____ Confirm honeymoon plans.

_____ Confirm wedding-night hotel reservations.

_____ Get all incoming guests' arrival times at airports and train stations.

_____ Arrange for transportation of guests to their hotel.

_____ Arrange for transportation needs of guests throughout the wedding weekend.

_____ Make beauty appointment for wedding day.

_____ Visit your hairstylist to "practice" with hairstyles for the big day.

_____ Get pre-wedding haircut, dye, or highlights.

_____ Go for fittings of your dress.

_____ Bride and groom pick up wedding bands.

_____ Attend showers.

_____ Send thank-yous to anyone who helped with the shower you hosted.

_____ Call wedding guests who have not RSVP'd to get the final head count.

_____ Help make up seating chart for reception.

_____ Write up seating place cards and table numbers.

_____ Pick up honeymoon travel tickets and information books (if honeymoon is your gift; otherwise, bride and groom do this).

_____ Make up welcome gift baskets for guests.

_____ Purchase gifts for couple and others.

_____ Wrap and label gifts.

_____ Arrange for wedding-day transportation for the bridal party and other guests if they will not be in limos.

_____ Purchase unity candle.

_____ Purchase garters (two—one for keeping, one for tossing).

_____ Purchase toasting flutes.

_____ Purchase cake knife.

_____ Purchase guest book.

_____ Purchase post-wedding toss-its (birdseed, flower petals, bubbles, bells, and so on) and decorate or personalize small containers, if you so choose.

_____ Purchase disposable wedding cameras.

One Week Before the Wedding

_____ Confirm all wedding plans with all wedding vendors.

     _____ Caterer (give final head count now)

     _____ Florist (give delivery instructions now)

     _____ Cake baker

     _____ Photographer

     _____ Videographer

     _____ Lighting technician

     _____ Ceremony musicians

     _____ Reception entertainers

     _____ Officiant

     _____ Ceremony site manager

     _____ Reception site manager

     _____ Wedding coordinator

     _____ Limousine company (give directions now)

     _____ Rental company agent

_____ Pay final deposits for all services.

_____ Place tips and fees in marked envelopes for participants such as the officiant, ceremony musicians, valets, and so on

_____ If supplying your own beverages, go (with plenty of assistants) to the local discount liquor and beverage supply house to make purchases.

_____ Drop off guest welcome baskets at hotel.

_____ Groom picks up tux.

_____ Groom and ushers pick up tux accessories, socks, shoes, and so on.

_____ Pack for any travel to be done.

_____ Break in your wedding-day shoes.

_____ Remind groom to get new shoes for the wedding day.

_____ Remind groom to get a haircut for the wedding day.

_____ Arrange for house- and pet-sitters for yourselves or for the couple.

_____ Notify the local police department of your upcoming absence, so that they can patrol your neighborhood.

_____ Get travelers' checks (if you so choose).

_____ Plan wedding day brunch, and inform bridal party and guests about it.

_____ Plan your special toasts.

_____ Prepare wedding announcements, which should be mailed the day after the wedding.

_____ Options: Attend bachelor's/bachelorette's party (if co-ed, or just join the girls).

The Day Before the Wedding

_____ Supervise delivery of rental items to wedding location.

_____ Supervise setup of all items at wedding location.

_____ Bride and groom finish packing suitcases and carry-ons for wedding night and honeymoon.

_____ For you and for bride and groom to remember: Stock your bag with your car keys, house keys, IDs, marriage license, wedding night and honeymoon hotel confirmations, medications, ATM card, and so on.

_____ Arrange for someone to leave the bride and groom's car, with their suitcases in the trunk, in the wedding-night hotel's parking lot for use the next day.

_____ Lay out all wedding-day clothes and accessories.

_____ Very important: Discuss with all residents in your home the bathroom schedule for the next day.

_____ Hand out printed directions to all family members and bridal-party members.

_____ Confirm when attendants need to show up on the wedding day and where to go.

_____ Arrange for a reliable relative to transport wedding gifts to the couple's home for safekeeping.

_____ Arrange for host to be in charge of handing out payment envelopes.

_____ Go to ATM so you have cash on hand for emergencies, tips, valet, and so on.

_____ Assemble emergency bag with extra stockings, lipstick, pressed powder, emery boards, and so on.

_____ Put a cell phone in the emergency bag.

_____ Put gas in the cars.

_____ Go to the beauty salon to get waxed and tweezed.

_____ Stock up on supplies for wedding-morning breakfast.

_____ Place final call to caterer or coordinator to answer last-minute questions.

_____ Attend rehearsal.

_____ Attend rehearsal dinner.

_____ Get a good night's sleep!

On the Wedding Day

_____ Set out favors and place cards at reception site, if manager will not be doing it.

_____ Set out post-wedding toss-its at ceremony site.

_____ Set out guest book and pen.

_____ Attend bridal brunch.

_____ Have hair and nails done at beauty salon, and have a massage if there's enough time.

_____ Have photos taken at home.

_____ Double-check that someone responsible has arranged for the couple's suitcases to go to their hotel room or in the car that will be taking them to the airport.

_____ Double-check that the appropriate people have the wedding rings for transport to the ceremony.

_____ Make sure the bag with your car keys, house keys, IDs, and other essential items travels with you to the wedding.

_____ Dress for the wedding.

_____ Help spouse or partner get dressed for the wedding.

_____ Help bride get dressed for the wedding.

_____ Pose for pictures.

_____ Attend the wedding.

_____ Attend the after-parties.

_____ Have a safe ride home!

The Day After the Wedding

_____ Have someone supervise the rental company's cleanup of the site, if necessary.

_____ Get a signed receipt for the return of all rented items.

_____ Have tuxes returned to rental store.

_____ Hold day-after breakfast or brunch for guests and bridal party.

_____ Graciously accept all compliments on the wedding.

_____ Transport guests to airports, train stations, and so on, for their return trips.

_____ Hire cleaning service if your home was the site of the wedding festivities.

_____ Plan a getaway or relaxing day at the spa to congratulate yourself on a job well done!

Appendix 4

Tipping Chart

THE FOLLOWING are suggested tip amounts to be given at or after the wedding. Keep in mind that these are suggestions, and you're free to reward your experts more generously if their service was above and beyond the call of duty:

Site manager: 15 to 20 percent of entire bill for reception

Valets: $1 per car

Waiters: $20 to $40 each, depending upon quality of service

Bartenders: 15 percent of liquor bill

Coat check: $1 per coat

Limousine drivers: 15 to 20 percent of transportation bill (Check to see if tip is already included in the contract first! If so, then on-the-day tip may be a smaller token.)

Delivery workers: $10 each if just dropping items off, $20 each if dropping off and setting up; more if they're transporting a lot of items

Tent assemblers and rental agency assemblers: $20 each

Entertainers: $25 to $30 each

Beauticians and barbers: 15 to 20 percent of beauty-salon bill

Cleanup crew: $20 each

Baby-sitters: $30 to $40 each, plus a gift, in addition to their hourly wages; more if baby-sitter is putting in extra hours or caring for several children

Event planner: 10 to 20 percent of your bill, *depending on the terms of contract*

Officiants: $50 to $100 tip is usually expected as a "donation"

Ceremony site staff: $20 to $30 per person

Organists and ceremony musicians: $20 to $50, depending on length of service

Sample Menu

Printed with permission of Lifestyles Catering (www.lifestylescatering.com),
Courtesy of Kaye Lissy and Chef Keith Falco

Celebration Menus
2004

Honeymoon Hors d'Oeuvres Buffet

Domestic Cheese and Fruit Display
Offered with Assorted Crackers

Garden Vegetable Basket
Filled with Assorted Seasonal Vegetables
Offered with a Roasted Garlic Ranch Dipping Sauce

Assorted Cocktail Sandwiches
Smoked Turkey with Herb Mayo, Honey Baked Ham and Cheese with Dijon Mustard,
Roast Beef with Horseradish Cream, and Grilled Vegetables with Basil Pesto
(200 sandwiches)

Gourmet Meatballs with Hardwood Smoked Barbeque Sauce
(300 pieces)

Mediterranean Pasta Salad
Tossed with Basil Balsamic Vinaigrette

Add Additional Passed or Displayed Appetizers

Choose Three

Grilled Quesadillas
Smoked Chicken, Pork, or Roasted Vegetable
with Chipotle Cream

Fried Pork and Vegetable Potstickers
Served with Spicy Soy Sauce

Traditional Deviled Eggs

Assorted Mini-Quiches

Chicken or Beef Satays

Crispy Tortilla Chips and Salsa

Spanikopita
Spinach and Feta baked in Crispy
Phyllo Triangles

Buffalo-Style Hot Wings
with Carrots, Celery, and Bleu
Cheese Dressing

Stuffed Grape Leaves

Fried Egg Rolls

Coconut Shrimp

Mini-Beef Wellingtons

Brunch Buffet

Included on All Buffets
Sausage Links and Crispy Bacon, Herb Roasted Baby Red Potatoes,
and Assorted Breakfast Breads to include Mini-Muffins, Sweet Breads,
Mini-Croissants, and Danish

Assorted Juices: Apple, Cranberry, and Orange

Station 1
Choose One:
French Toast Sticks, Waffles, or Blintzes
All served with Warm Maple Syrup, Strawberry Coulis, and Powdered Sugar

Yogurt Bar with Vanilla and Berry Yogurt and Granola

or

Fresh Fruit Display

Station 2

Choose One:
Assorted Quiches, Spiral Baked Ham, Smoked Turkey, or Eggs Benedict

Greek Spinach Salad
Baby Spinach Leaves, Diced Roma Tomatoes, Sliced Cucumbers, Kalamata Olives,
Red Onion, and Crumbled Feta Cheese
Tossed with Greek Vinaigrette

or

Brie en Croute
Whole Brie Cheese, Wrapped in Puff Pastry,
Filled with either Sautéed Forest Mushrooms or Dried Cranberries, Apples, and Walnuts

Complimentary Drizzled Strawberries

Resources

(The following information is provided to help with research only. Neither the author nor the publisher endorses any company listed in the Resources section. At the time of publication, all phone numbers and Web sites were current. We apologize if any changes have been made by the time this book gets to you.)

Wedding-Planning Web Sites

Bliss Weddings: blissweddings.com
Bridal Guide: www.bridalguide.com
Bride's: www.brides.com
Della Weddings: www.dellaweddings.com
Elegant Bride: www.elegantbridemagazine.com
The Knot: www.theknot.com
Modern Bride: www.modernbride.com

Martha Stewart Weddings: www.marthastewart.com
Town and Country Weddings: www.tncweddings.com
Weddings Bells: www.weddingbells.com
Wedding Channel: www.weddingchannel.com
Weddingpages: www.weddingpages.com
Wed Net: www.wednet.com

Wedding Wear

Gowns

After Six: (800) 444-8304,
www.aftersix.com

Alfred Angelo: (800) 531-1125,
www.alfredangelo.com

Bianchi: (800) 669-2346

Bill Levkoff: (800) LEVKOFF [538-5633],
www.billlevkoff.com

Bridal Originale: (618) 345-4499
www.silhouettesmaids.com

Chadwick's of Boston Special Occasions:
(800) 525-6650

Champagne Formals: (212) 302-9162,
www.champagneformals.com

David's Bridal: (888) 480-BRIDE [2743],
www.davidsbridal.com

Dessy Creations: (800) 52-DESSY [523-3779],
www.dessy.com

Galina: (212) 564-1020,
www.galinabridals.com

Group USA: (877) 867-7600,
www.groupusa.com

JC Penney: (800) 322-1189,
www.jcpenney.com

Jessica McClintock: (800) 333-5301,
www.jessicamcclintock.com

Jim Hjelm Occasions: (800) 686-7880,
www.jimhjelmoccasions.com

Lazaro: (212) 764-5781,
www.lazarobridal.com

Macy's: (877) 622-9274,
www.macys.weddingchannel.com

Melissa Sweet Bridal: (404) 633-4395,
www.melissasweet.com

Mori Lee: (212) 840-5070,
www.morileeinc.com

Roaman's Romance (plus sizes):
(800) 436-0800

Spiegel: (800) 474-555, www.spiegel.com

Vera Wang: (800) VEW-VERA [839-8372],
www.verawang.com

Watters and Watters: (972) 960-9884,
www.watters.com

Shoes and Accessories

Shoes and Handbags

David's Bridal: (888) 480-BRIDE [2743],
www.davidsbridal.com

Dyeables: (800) 431-2000,
www.dyeables.com

Fenaroli for Regalia: (617) 350-6556,
www.fenaroli.com

Kenneth Cole: 800-KENCOLE [536-2653]

Nina Footwear: (800) 233-NINA [6562],
www.ninashoes.com

Salon Shoes: (650) 588-8677,
www.salonshoes.com

Watters and Watters: (972) 960-9884,
www.watters.com

Jewelry

American Gem Society: (702) 255-6500,
www.ags.org
Benchmark: (800) 633-5950,
www.benchmarkrings.com
Bianca: 213-622-7234,
www.BiancaPlatinum.com
Blue Nile: (800) 242-2728, www.bluenile.com
Cartier: (800) CARTIER [227-8437],
www.cartier.com
Christian Bauer: (800) 228-3724,
www.christianbauer.com
DeBeers: www.debeers.com
European Gemological Society:
(877) EGL-USA-1 [345-8721],
www.egl.co.za
Honora: (888) 2HONORA [246-6672],
www.honora.com
Jeff Cooper Platinum: (888) 522-6222,
www.jeffcooperdesigns.com
Keepsake Diamond Jewelry:
(888) 4-KEEPSAKE [453-3772]

Lazare Diamond: www.lazarediamonds.com
Novell: (888) 916-6835,
www.novelldesignstudio.com
OGI Wedding Bands Unlimited:
(800) 578-3846, www.ogi-ltd.com
Paul Klecka: (888) P-KLECKA
[755-3252], www.klecka.com
Rudolf Erdel Platinum: (888) 945-4356,
www.rudolferdel.com
Scott Kay Platinum: (800) 487-4898,
www.scottkay.com
Tiffany: (800) 526-0649, www.tiffany.com
Wedding Ring Hotline:
(800) 985-RING [7464],
www.weddingringhotline.com
Zales: (800) 311-JEWEL [5393],
www.zales.com

For information on how to design
your own rings, check out
www.adiamondisforever.com

Wedding Supplies and Services

Books and Planners

Amazon.com: www.amazon.com
Barnes and Noble: (800) 242-6657,
www.bn.com
Borders: www.borders.com

Cake Supplies

Wilton: (800) 794-5866, www.wilton.com

Invitations

An Invitation to Buy—Nationwide:
www.invitations4sale.com
Anna Griffin Invitation Design:
(888) 817-8170, www.annagriffin.com
Botanical PaperWorks: (877) 956-7393,
www.botanicalpaperworks.com
Camelot Wedding Stationery: (800) 280-2860

Crane and Co.: (800) 572-0024,
www.crane.com

Evangel Christian Invitations: (800) 457-9774, www.evangelwedding.com

Invitations by Dawn: (800) 257-9567,
www.invitationsbydawn.com

Julie Holcomb Printers: (510) 654-6416,
www.julieholcombprinters.com

Now and Forever: (800) 521-0584,
www.now-and-forever.com

PaperStyle.com (ordering invitations online):
(888) 670-5300, www.paperstyle.com

Papyrus: (800) 886-6700,
www.papyrusonline.com

Precious Collection: (800) 537-5222,
www.preciouscollection.com

PSA Essentials: (248) 288-7584,
www.psaessentials.com

Renaissance Writings: (800) 246-8483,
www.RenaissanceWriting.com

Rexcraft: (800) 635-3898,
www.rexcraft.com

Vismara Invitations: (303) 378-4921,
www.vismarainvitations.com

Willow Tree Lane: (800) 219-1022,
www.willowtreelane.com

Flowers

About.com: www.about.com

Association of Special Cut Flowers:
(440) 774-2887

Flowersales.com: www.flowersales.com

Flowerweb: www.flowerweb.com

Romantic Flowers:
www.romanticflowers.com

Photo Albums

Exposures Online: (800) 222-4947,
www.exposuresonline.com

Wine and Champagne

Wine.com: (800) 289-6886, www.wine.com

Wine-Searcher: www.winesearcher.com

Wine Spectator: www.winespectator.com

Weather Sites

For checking the weather at your ceremony, reception, or honeymoon sites, including five to ten day forecasts, and weather bulletins for storms, tides, boating, and golf:

AccuWeather: www.accuweather.com

Rain or Shine: 5-day forecasts,
plus ski and boating conditions:
www.rainorshine.com

Sunset Time: (precise sunset time for any day of the year) www.usno.navy.mil [*Check this out if you're planning an outdoor wedding and want to time your ceremony for sunset!*]

Weather Channel: www.weather.com

Warehouse Stores

BJ's Wholesale Club: www.bjs.com
Costco: www.costco.com

Sam's Club: www.samsclub.com

Paper Supplies
(for printing programs, place cards, invitations, and so on)

Paper Access: (800) 727-3701,
    www.paperaccess.com
Paper Direct: (800) A-PAPERS [272-7377],
    www.paperdirect.com
Staples: (800) 3STAPLE [378-2753],
    www.staples.com

USABride: (800) 781-9129,
    www.usabrideweddings.com
Ultimate Wedding Store: (800) 300-5587,
    www.ultimatewedding.com/store
Wedmart.com: (888) 802-2229,
    www.wedmart.com

Beauty and Health

Avon: www.avon.com
Bobbi Brown Essentials: (877) 310-9222,
    www.bobbibrown.com
Clinique: (800) 419-4041,
    www.clinique.com
Elizabeth Arden: www.elizabetharden.com
Estée Lauder: (877) 311-3883,
    www.esteelauder.com
iBeauty: www.ibeauty.com
Lancôme: (800) LANCOME [526-2663],
    www.lancome.com
L'Oréal: www.loreal.com
Mac: (800) 588-0070,
    www.maccosmetics.com

Makeover Studio: www.makeoverstudio.com
    (choose your face shape and experiment
    with makeup shades and looks)
Max Factor: www.maxfactor.com
Maybelline: www.maybelline.com
Neutrogena: www.neutrogena.com
Pantene: (800) 224-9490, www.pantene.com
Reflect.com (customized beauty products):
    www.reflect.com
Rembrandt (tooth-whitening products):
    www.rembrandt.com
Revlon: www.revlon.com
Sephora: www.sephora.com

Index